Sarah Lee

Lavinia Greenlaw is a novelist and poet who has also written opera libretti, songs, and radio plays. She was once in a band. She lives in London and is a professor of creative writing at the University of East Anglia.

ALSO BY LAVINIA GREENLAW

Fiction

*Mary George of Allnorthover*
*An Irresponsible Age*

Poetry

*Night Photograph*
*A World Where News Travelled Slowly*
*Thoughts of a Night Sea* (with Garry Fabian Miller)
*Minsk*

# *The*
# IMPORTANCE
# *of* MUSIC
# *to* GIRLS

# ❋ *The* ❋ IMPORTANCE *of* MUSIC *to* GIRLS

Lavinia Greenlaw

PICADOR

FARRAR, STRAUS AND GIROUX

*New York*

THE IMPORTANCE OF MUSIC TO GIRLS. Copyright © 2007 by Lavinia Greenlaw. All rights reserved. Printed in the United States of America. For information, address Picador, 175 Fifth Avenue, New York, N.Y. 10010.

www.picadorusa.com

Picador® is a U.S. registered trademark and is used by Farrar, Straus and Giroux under license from Pan Books Limited.

For information on Picador Reading Group Guides, please contact Picador.
E-mail: readinggroupguides@picadorusa.com

Grateful acknowledgment is made to Jon Savage for permission to reprint an extract from his review of Joy Division's *Unknown Pleasures*, which originally appeared in *Melody Maker*, July 21, 1979, and is included in his book *Time Travel: From the Sex Pistols to Nirvana* (Vintage, 1997).

*Designed by Cassandra J. Pappas*

ISBN-13: 978-0-312-42837-2
ISBN-10: 0-312-42837-5

Originally published by Faber and Faber Limited, Great Britain

First published in the United States by
Farrar, Straus and Giroux

First Picador Edition: June 2009

10  9  8  7  6  5  4  3  2  1

*for Georgia Elizabeth*

*leaving home*

This is a work of memory—facts have been altered.
Names have been changed.

# Contents

# *The* IMPORTANCE *of* MUSIC *to* GIRLS

# MY PAPA'S WALTZ

*The hand that held my wrist*
*Was battered on one knuckle;*
*At every step you missed*
*My right ear scraped a buckle.*
　　　—THEODORE ROETHKE,
　　　　"My Papa's Waltz"

I remember the dancing of my earliest years in silence, as about the body alone. My father must have hummed a tune as I stood on his shoes and he waltzed me, but what I remember are the giant steps I was suddenly making. The world rose up under one foot and pushed my body to one side as that foot set off in a high violent arc. I didn't know if I was going to be able to follow but at the last moment the world gathered up the rest of me. And so it went on: the world pulled and shoved while I lurched and stretched.

This was not a gentle game, which was why we four children loved it. We liked to be thrown about—by a roller coaster, slide, or swing, in a rough sea, on a trampoline, or by grown-ups who in moving us at their force and speed gave us a taste of the di-

4 Lavinia Greenlaw

mensions of adult life. We had a young uncle who played less carefully than my father. He would take me by the hands and spin me around like a tea cloth full of wet lettuce until I thought my arms would be wrenched from their sockets. As the pain bunched in my shoulders and my brain shrank, I was amazed that such movement was possible. I wasn't scared. I knew that I could break and had an idea of what it felt like to break, but I also knew I wasn't going to.

The waltz was more interesting than other such games because its force had to be met. It depended upon the tension between trying not to move and letting yourself be moved. I trod down hard on my father's shoes, braced my arms, and dug my nails into his shirt cuffs like someone finding a hold on a cliff. This is the starting point of dance: something—the music, the steps, your partner—holds you but you also have to hold it and, to achieve the necessary tension, hold yourself *against* it.

A lot of my childhood was about being held back or slowed down. It took hours to leave the house, as to get us all ready, and keep us ready, was like trying to keep four plates spinning. Someone lost a glove or refused their coat, was cross or hungry or needed a clean diaper. We spent a lot of time waiting—to be delivered or collected, for the school day to end or the night to be over. We moved in caravan formation and at the speed of camels, taking two days to drive the 250 miles from London to the west coast of Wales, pottering along in a pair of Morris Travellers.

Once released, we were fizzy and impatient. If something was high we climbed it and jumped off; if it was steep we hurtled down it on cycles, sleds, or trays. We ran or rolled down any hill we came to regardless of nettles, glass, dog shit, or stones. If the landscape filled up with rain, leaves, fog, or snow, we continued to move through it as fast as we could, not fearing what might now be concealed.

Every now and then the world gathered itself in refusal. I

slammed into it and got hurt. At four, I went down a slide suck-
ing on a bamboo garden cane, which hit the ground before I
did. The top two inches jammed into the roof of my mouth, and
I stood over a basin and watched it fill up with blood, feeling
nothing, interested only in my sister offering me a teddy bear she
would not normally part with. When I woke up after the operation to remove the piece of cane, I was curious only about the
coal fire opposite my bed and the taste of hospital ice cream.

For a long time, this accident was just something that had
happened to my mouth. Other people had to make the connections for me.

"That cane was lodged very close to your brain," my mother
later said. "We could tell you were more or less all right but the
surgeons didn't know if they could remove it without doing any
damage."

My brother added, "It's why people shoot themselves that
way."

"And it could have affected your speech," continued my
mother, "by changing the shape of the roof of your mouth."

Being pushed out of shape made me realize that I had a
shape to return to, like my toy cat who sat on a drum and whose
parts were kept in tension by elastic. If I pressed the underside of
the drum, the cat fell to its knees or slumped to one side. I let go
and the cat sprang to one side as if jiving. I was fascinated by the
instant way it changed shape and then snapped back, and by the
ambiguity of its bright little face—so eager to please and yet so
imperturbable.

My body had felt like that of the toy cat, an arrangement of
parts. I would watch my hand touch the bar of an electric fire or
my foot tread on a nail, and discover that they belonged to me. I
now knew that my mouth shaped my voice and that my brain was
right there, just above it. I saw this most clearly thirty years later
on an X-ray, which showed that instead of arching back to cradle

my skull, the vertebrae at the top of my spine thrust my head forward. In that accident, my head had been thrown back so abruptly that it had been compensating ever since, leaving me with the feeling of being precipitate, of tipping into rather than entering the next moment, thought, or sentence.

So the body adds up and the world reminds you of the body's limits, although it can be surprisingly kind. At eight I jumped through a window, and I can still remember how the glass billowed and held me before it exploded. I was midair, I had escaped the person I was running away from, and I was being held. Nothing has seemed as peaceful since. I stepped out of that ring of shattered glass like a corpse from a chalk silhouette and walked away with a cut on each knee.

These collisions with the world taught me its substance and laws as well as my own. I had danced before I knew what my body was, and did not understand what moved me. It was not music yet.

# DAPPLES AND GRAYS

*Or a woman's voice sang and reached a little
beyond expectation . . .*
—RAINER MARIA RILKE,
"The Vast Night"

The women in our family have one voice. People cannot tell my mother, sister, daughter, and me apart on the telephone. Sometimes I play back the answering machine and think I have left a message for myself. When it comes to singing, though, my mother's glassy soprano stands apart. The rest of us have dry, deep singing voices. We strain in church and at carol concerts; as the descant rises, we crack and hold off and concentrate on the underpinning.

My mother never raised her voice. A doctor, she was clinically pragmatic. When she dislocated a finger, she set it herself. When there wasn't time to bake a cake, she served up the raw mixture for pudding. When she couldn't get four children to stay in bed at night, she used our toddler harnesses to strap us in. (There were times when we cried out to remind her, "Reins! Reins!") She had a lucidity that was dazzling and liberating but in some ways too clear. Sometimes I did not want to see more than I expected.

Even when the question has been formulated, it can be impossible to ask. My mother was so private and I felt so conditioned not to know her that it would not have occurred to me to ask whom she'd had lunch with, let alone how she was. Yet we reveal something of our nature when we sing, something that can be disguised in our speaking voice. It's as if we are opening the door to an inner acoustic, and the acoustic of my mother's voice was absolute space. When she sang me to sleep I felt at peace, but it was like being settled into emptiness. I felt love and unboundedness, and whenever I sing, those are the sensations that arise.

What we sing to a child who is too young to sing along is perhaps as undirected as what we sing to ourselves. My mother's singing was not a plaint, but the arrested atmosphere of "Greensleeves" or "Scarborough Fair" was clearer to me in her tone than it ever was once I understood the words. While I was still too young to follow a story I held on to details, which her voice laid out with forensic care (my father had first seen her in the dissection room of their medical school, cutting up a body): a long boat, a narrow street, a cambric shirt, all the pretty little horses.

Folk songs, show tunes, and sea shanties were freed of their theatrics, their images clarified into light and shadow. "What Shall We Do with the Drunken Sailor?" had not a whiff of rum, sea salt, or jolly Jack Tar about it. For me, it hung on the line "Put him in the longboat till he's sober." I saw the tall side of a ship, the drop into the dark, the deep water, and somewhere out there, not adrift but apart, a place of punishment or rest—which, I couldn't tell. In "Cockles and Mussels," Molly Malone "wheeled her wheelbarrow through streets broad and narrow," and this again is what held my attention—the small girl and the towering houses: the idea of a journey through the dark alone. I was fascinated by the oddly somber "Pretty Little Horses," and when my mother sang of those "Blacks and bays, dapples and grays," they rippled across my mind as elusively as sun on water. Elsewhere, I conjured substance out of sound: the "cambric shirt" of "Scarborough Fair," roughly hemmed with two hard *c*'s that stuck in the throat; or the stretchy length of the trailing "Greensleeves" on which that song repeatedly tugged.

Before we were old enough to catch the bus, my mother drove us to school, sometimes still in her dressing gown. My swaddled baby brother rolled around in the back while we older ones squabbled and she sang, "Who will buy this wonderful morning? Such a sky you never did see . . ." I realize that this might have been ironic. Then again, she could have been trying to get us to notice that it *was* a wonderful morning.

We don't sing when we're feeling harassed. Her singing was part of her coolness, like the cool white hand she placed on my cheek to wake me each morning and the cool way she held me when I was in a frenzy, as if she were marble and I were bubbling mud. It was part of the hauteur with which she carried herself, so you knew that if the car broke down and she had to walk across London in that frilly sky-blue dressing gown she would do so gloriously. She still had the regal posture of a debutante, and above all she wouldn't give a damn. Just as she would do anything for us, she would do anything.

This sung world was serene in its truthfulness and without comfort. It sent me off into space and, from early on, the idea of deep space became a source of consolation. I closed my eyes and trusted my mother's voice even as it seemed to let me go, because I understood that it was releasing me as an act of love.

# A CLOUD STRUCK BY
# LIGHTNING

*The cat went here and there*
*And the moon spun round like a top,*
*And the nearest kin of the moon,*
*The creeping cat looked up.*
—W. B. YEATS,
"The Cat and the Moon"

When I was so young that like a cat I was oblivious to mirrors, I sang and danced for myself.

I was the second of four children and grew up in the city, and so much of life was movement and noise. If I sang or danced, something of life took shape.

Was I a noisy child? I made noise as a way of bringing people toward me but also to see them off. How were they supposed to tell which I intended? How was I? Was this a war cry or a love song? A display of grace or a show of strength? Ugly or beautiful? We four kept up our noise as a form of vigilance. It was the sound of rocks banged together, shields drummed by swords, boots stamping, jet planes swooping. How much song and dance have come out of just this?

My family held me. It was complicated but strong, a machine that made life happen so that I didn't have to. It protected me too. Until I was eleven or so, I was not made to take on substance.

I had as much capacity for delight as for fear and did not experience any unusual trauma. It was a matter of impact. *All* experience was trauma.

I liked our noise yet came to find the volume of life too high, and as I couldn't turn it down, turned myself down instead. Before then, I felt like a cloud struck by lightning. This was how someone once described being in love to me, and it could be said that in terms of how the world acted upon me, I was in love.

# ALL WOUND CLOSE IN A RING

*Sometimes all wound close in a ring, to which as*
*    fast they spunne*
*As any wheele a Turner makes, being tried how it*
*    will runne*
*While he is set; and out againe, as full of speed,*
*    they wound,*
*Not one left fast or breaking hands.*
                                        —HOMER,
                                        *The Iliad,* Book 18

W hen children meet other children, they have to do something—fight or play. Our games were disordered, their rules the subject of further meta-games. We four were born each twenty months apart and so these games were also predicated upon wanting to kill one another. I persuaded my older brother to climb onto an aerial railway when I knew the seat was unhooked. He flipped over and fell, cracking his head open on the path below. He would dare me to eat a wasp, climb onto a roof, jump out of a tree, confident that I could not refuse. When we had construction, my little brother made a game of throwing bricks at the rest of us. My sister was quieter and more frightening. As I sat reading in a chair, she liked to inch silently across the room and then throttle me.

Four was in any case an uncomfortable number. Two people can dance alone and a roomful of people can dance together. Six people make a decent-size ring. But can you imagine four people dancing? It would look awkward—halfway between intimacy and an occasion. Whereas two is concentrated opposition, three cleanly unbalanced, and five rich with possible alignments, four is too obvious. The only way to achieve tension within it is three to one, and I, being too close to my older brother to want to admire him and too close to the younger ones to be admired, was the one.

When I was five and started school, I had to give up fighting as a way of expressing myself. It was around this time that dance became a dangerous thing. At school I had to sit still and be quiet, stand up when a teacher came into the room, walk on the left in the corridor, go to the lavatory only at break, sit cross-legged with arms folded during assembly, queue to enter a room, queue to leave, queue for lunch, raise my hand and wait to be given permission to eat or speak. I was bewildered. I did not know how to order myself, how to exercise that amount of control.

It was even harder to master the rules of playground games: not words and steps, those I picked up quickly, but the nuances. These games involved attentiveness and coordination, which were not only physical but social. I had no idea how to make friends, having relied until now on the scrum of my siblings to overpower or exclude any other children we met. I felt held in place by them despite our battles, and had little need for anyone else. And then I did: at school, I suddenly wanted my own world and my own people to go in it. The children I looked to were those who had already found their place, formed their circle and closed it. To have friends, I had to break into a ring.

I already knew circle dances such as "Ring-a-Ring o' Roses" and "Here We Go Round the Mulberry Bush," but I had no idea how potent they were. In a playground full of girls, the circles were large. If you were not part of the discussion in which the circle was proposed then you had to rush in while it was being formed. Once all hands were held, the circle was closed. You might hover on the edge and hope for someone to stumble and create an opening or, if you felt more confident, you might tap someone on the shoulder or tug their sleeve. Once you were in, you had to keep up and there would always be someone older, taller, and sharper who was going to move the circle faster or send it into reverse. They might add extra rules, gestures, or steps. You had to keep up.

I don't remember the songs to which we danced these circles. We were not interested in what the words might mean, and they were so familiar that they had become abstracted into a rhythm and a set of cues, like conversation. Being in the circle was a perfect state. I was invisible but component, moving but held. I didn't have to talk to anyone, no one was looking at me but I was at the heart of things. The faster we went, the tighter we held on to one another until we knew that if we let go we would all fall down, but while we kept hold, we might be flying. The song lost shape or wore itself out through sheer repetition. We grew lighter as our breath grew heavier until we were just that, breath—released, ecstatic.

For the first time I understood that belonging was a way of escaping myself and of finding a place in the world: the blur of the round-and-round, the speed at which each member of the ring becomes indistinct, where nothing can be seen anymore so all is felt, and difference flattens into figures on a vase.*

*This is what Homer described as *khoreia* (which gives us choreography), the dance in a ring in which everyone is equally component and the thing is its own momentum like the wheel set to run downhill. Homer is describing a detail on a vase, so the ring is doubly a ring—fixed in itself and fixed in the circle of clay.

I could keep up, but I did not belong because I had not learned to contain myself within the figure I was making. Nervous, furious, and barely aware of myself, I drove other people away. I was tolerated on the edge of the circle until one day the leader announced that I was not to be included anymore. She proposed this as she might a new game: "I know, let's . . ." and the other girls followed her to the opposite side of the playground. Usually, something like that would send me into a rage of rejection. I once hit someone for not wanting to be my friend. But something came to me that day in the playground, and as the ring closed without me, I made to step outside it and took myself off and made myself busy within a ring of my own imagining. Quickly, the girls returned and invited me back. I accepted and the whole thing was passed off as nothing more than a dance.

School was a series of rings: friends, gender, class, and year as well as classroom, building, playground, grounds. The doors and gates were always unlocked, but it seemed inconceivable to pass through them at other than the permitted times. One day I made a paper lion. For once it looked like what I had hoped for, and the teacher was pleased. The bell rang and I rushed out to the school gates clutching the lion, desperate to show my mother what I had done. She wasn't there so I waited, with such intentness that I didn't take in the fact that no one else was around. When I eventually realized this, panic soared—where was my mother? Then I looked about and the thought became Where is everyone? I looked and looked, and it became Where am I? The building and playground behind me were quiet. In front of me was a weekday grown-up London I did not know. Eventually I understood that the bell I'd heard had only been for break and that the rest of the morning's lessons were now taking place.

In my hurtling excitement, I had compressed the day. I was on the edge of school and no one appeared to have noticed. I looked back at the school and it seemed as impenetrable and re-mote as the city in front of me. I was nowhere, a point from which I could step in or out, forward or back.

I don't remember how I returned to my classroom that day but know that I must have done so. The experience, though, had offered a possibility I could not let go of. Not long afterward, I decided, aged six, that I wanted to go home. I walked out of the gates, along the road, across Hampstead Heath, up the hill, and rang the front-door bell. It was so simple that when my mother opened the door I could not understand what hit her, and it was as if something had hit her—as if by stepping out of place, I had stepped into her.

# PLAINE AND EASIE RULES

*The lines, which a number of people together form, in country or figure dancing, make a delightful play upon the eye, especially when the whole figure is to be seen at one view, as at the playhouse from a gallery . . . [T]he dances of barbarians are often represented without these movements, being only composed of wild skipping, jumping, and turning around, or running backward and forward with convulsive shrugs, and distorted gestures.*

—WILLIAM HOGARTH,
*Analysis of Beauty*

I don't know what's become of Hampstead," my great-grandmother once remarked. "It's full of Turks and infidels." She lived (and is buried) on the city's rim, at the top of the hill on which Hampstead is built. I was almost born around the corner but at the last minute my parents moved down the other side of the hill into a flat in a house that had been built by Evelyn Waugh's father. Unlovely, it sat bang on the line between the postcodes NW3 and NW11, bohemian Hamp-

stead and suburban Golders Green, or what Robert Lowell's
mother called, in terms of her own Boston geography, "barely
perched on the outer rim of the hub of decency."*

Our address was one of several aspects of our lives that resis-
ted the expectations of our class and through which we stepped
out of line. The general rule was that you could live in the wrong
place so long as your house had charm. My parents were more
gung-ho, and my mother somewhat resistant to the aesthetics she
had been born into. We grew up in a confusion of shabbiness
and beauty, thinking of possessions as there to be worn out or
given away, and found ourselves lighter but emptier than we
might have expected.

Our lives faced into the city, where my father's medical practice was in Camden Town. My father was most alive in that landscape, a place so various and full of things for a doctor to do. He
looked after the homeless alcoholics who slept at Arlington
House, as well as young actors, architects, and writers, some of
whom became famous. We ate croissants, dolmades, and pickled
herrings, and brewed Turkish coffee in a brass pot. One of the
handsome young brothers from Trattoria Lucca opposite the surgery brought over cappuccino on a tray held high on the tips of
his fingers above the traffic; his mother, Mrs. Boggi, gave me
chocolate and pinched my cheek. The local baker took us into
his kitchens, where I was made delirious by the warm and sugary
air. We bought paper twists of blue-tinged North Sea shrimps
from a man who sold them in Flask Walk outside the (by then
very smart) house in which he'd been born.

We loafed around market stalls and canal locks, and walked
the dog on Primrose Hill at dusk just as the wolves in the zoo began to howl. The dog would howl back. I stood there in the dark
with my father, in silence, and knew that we were both sad, that

---

*Robert Lowell, "Revere Street," *Life Studies*, 1956.

we could not speak of it and that we each drew something from the dark. I looked down onto a lit city that could not be tidied into circles or lines, and felt at home.

It seems strange now that in such a place as Camden Town I could have been taught English country dancing. My lessons took place at Cecil Sharp House, the headquarters of the English Folk Dance and Song Society. This kind of dancing was like gambling for matchsticks rather than money. It had no charge and I felt no flight or spring or joy but trailed around in a swill of children, learning patterns and steps that seemed even less interesting than the playground games I was beginning to grow out of. I was no longer prepared to jump and clap whenever music presented itself, but needed to be persuaded.

We fumbled along, trying to master the reel or "hey," in which two lines or circles of people move past each other in opposite directions in a kind of plait. The music sagged (Where did the music come from? A gramophone?) as we children made flabby circles and limp lines, and bumped into one another as one pair set off with a spurt into "Heel and Toe," only to crash immediately into their neighbors who were still trying to work out which foot to put down when and where.

Cecil Sharp drew heavily upon John Playford's 1651 publication, *The English Dancing Master, or, Plaine and Easie Rules for the Dancing of Country Dances with the Tunes to each Dance.* Playford claimed that "*Plato*, that Famous Philosopher thought it meet, that young Ingenious Children be taught to dance." His dances sound passionate and complicated: "Every Lad His Lass"—a triple-minor set; "The Friar in the Well, or The Maid Peeped Out at the Window"—longways for as many as will; "Dissembling Heart, or The Lost Love"—longways for six; "Fain I Would"— square for eight; "The Collier's Daughter, or, The Duke of Rutland's Delight"—triple-minor set.

Later, I would do some fierce country dancing at ceilidhs and weddings, and would see what it could be used for. At seven, I was impatient and unimpressed. We were taught to "honor" our partner at the beginning and end of each dance with a brief curtsey or bow, and did so drearily. I remember the passing impassive faces of the other children as we lined up, linked arms, clapped hands, skipped. There were no intricate steps or flamboyant gestures and you had to submit to your partner, to a four or an eight. We bumbled along while someone somewhere shouted instructions. The moves were homely—the cast or the basket. Even the promenade was only a measured stroll. Scottish, Irish, and Welsh country dancing involved costumes, stamping, rigid posture, and fine details. They danced among swords.

I gave up on Cecil Sharp and tried country dancing at a local school, where I had to wear a skirt covered with tiny green sprigs and a lacy white blouse with puff sleeves. The skirt stuck out from a crudely elasticated waist and the shirt scratched. There was something helplessly staid about the effect. I looked more like a great-aunt than a country maid, and not remotely frothy or verdant.

If this English dancing had any virtue, it was that it tried to be nice. It might have been dancing for people embarrassed about dancing. This was my national dance? Other people's involved smashing glasses or plates; they wore sashes, hats, tassels, scarves, and swirling skirts; they made noise. We were simply being conditioned, as in our sports days and Brownie troops, to *join in.*

My parents had both been miserably if well educated at boarding school and wanted for us a kind of social ease and equipment they felt they did not get: they wanted us to be able to join in the broader world. Joining in at my North London primary school was complicated by the fact that it had pupils from thirty or so different nationalities. There were automatic and visible allegiances as well as shared languages, food, and observances. My Jewish friends stayed in on Friday evenings and kept the Sabbath on Saturdays. They could speak Hebrew, Yiddish, and German. They had a separate assembly and weren't allowed to write the word *God*. My Spanish friend was Catholic and crossed herself elaborately. My other friends were Mauritian, Indian, and Japanese. I wasn't even Catholic. We had a parade each year in national dress, and I didn't have one so couldn't take part. I wasn't going to wear my lace blouse and flowery skirt.

For a while I declared myself "half Scottish, quarter Irish, and quarter Welsh." My grandfathers were Scottish, one by birth, the other by descent. I had a kilt in my mother's Mackintosh tartan and my brother a pair of Mackintosh shorts. That grandfather married a woman who brought into the family the wide face and eyes of, it was dancingly said, a "Mary Kelly of County Cork." My Greenlaw grandfather joined the Gordon Highlanders in the First World War, had his lip shot off, and endured some of the first plastic surgery. He had been training to be a classics teacher in Aberdeen and was one of only two in his class who returned from the war. Both gave up teaching and became doctors. His wife was the daughter of a Welsh Methodist minister.

This all-round Celticness gave me color; Englishness seemed to have no color at all. Only I wasn't Scottish, I was English. There was so much difference around me that I wanted my own, whereas my friends' parents, especially the Jews who had fled Europe, wanted their children to belong. Surnames were anglicized: Silberstein became Silver, Rosenkranz, Rose. My Spanish friend was restricted to one of her four or five surnames and her first name toned down from Maria to Mary. I, on the other hand, was taught how to dance a reel, to promenade and do-si-do, to heel and toe. Instead of Hogarth's barbaric wildness, I was learning through dance to be contained and regulated, and to have that great English form of beauty—to look *nice*.

## ❊ 6 ❊

# KORE

*The world had reached a point at which the econ-*
*omy of metamorphosis that had sustained it for so*
*long through the period of Zeus's adventures was*
*no longer enough. Things had lost their primordial*
*fluidity, had hardened into profile, and the game*
*that had once been played out between one shape*
*and another was now reduced to the mere alterna-*
*tion of appearance and disappearance. From now*
*on, it was a question not only of accepting life in a*
*single immutable form but of accepting the cer-*
*tainty that that form would one day disappear*
*without trace.*

— ROBERTO CALASSO,
*The Marriage of Cadmus and Harmony*

I was going to not be, and I would not be forever. Time spooled on and there I was, trapped on the wrong side of it. I went to wake my mother and she said something about sleep being a rehearsal, but as I was not good at sleep and had little sense of what it was for, this was no consolation. Further conversations with my mother opened up a gap between us. She believed in God. He had come to her at the same age as that sense of black time came to me. She spoke of death as if it were something to look forward to.

By the time I was eight, I was taking on a fixed shape. It was as if for years I had looked for myself and at last I was getting glimpses. This happened most clearly when I placed myself in opposition when arguing, evading, or in physical tension: swimming twenty lengths, climbing a tree, doing ballet. Ballet was something undertaken alone, and while you did not hold hands, as when dancing in a ring, it made you part of the body, the *corps*.

Ballet was tough and it hurt, but it gave me a way of ordering my body. I liked the precision, and the fact that there were always further refinements and tensions to be acquired. Ballet taught me about timing and consequence, and I remember it without music, a physical discipline, as a set of sequences or rites.

You start by standing still and then you learn how to stand. Next you learn how to move your feet through five positions, and then your arms. Next you learn how to move both simultaneously. Then you learn how to bend, how to rise, how to describe shapes in the air with your toe. Only then do you set off. I launched myself into each movement as precisely as I could and discovered that to remain still was the hardest movement of all.

Ballet also teaches you that each step or gesture is the outcome of another, a lesson I had already absorbed from Greek myth—the tumble of lover into foe, child into mother, girl into tree, god into swan. The sprawl of metamorphosis is the child state, one in which you can be stone or flower, suitor or captor, boy or girl, ancient or new in the space of a day. You are molten, multiple, perpetual, and so is time.

We were to perform the story of Persephone, who was first

called *Kore*, "girl,"* and, being the essence of girl, was the one that Hades, king of the underworld, wanted for his queen. Her mother Demeter's grief sent the earth into mourning and nothing grew. In the end Persephone was returned to her but, having eaten six pomegranate seeds while she was in the underworld, had to go back there for half the year. And so the cycle was fixed: spring and summer while Persephone was aboveground, autumn and winter when she disappeared.

Around this time, I had been walking home down the hill one day when I said aloud to myself that it did not matter where I was or what was going on around me, because I lived in my head. The habit of absenting myself was so strong that I eventually had no control over it. It happened in the midst of conversations, instructions, examinations. My imagined world was more vivid and more felt and I was part of it, no, the center of it. It felt like the place I belonged to and from where I had come. What was I doing here? Real life was abrasive, brutal, off-key. I did not know how to get it in proportion and so every encounter— whether it be with a story, a stranger, an insect, a piece of candy, the weather—was exhausting. I was exhausting too. My mother later remembered a time when I had food poisoning and the medicine I was given left me sweetly doped up: "You were so charming when you were sedated."

I knew I was Persephone, but to my astonishment was cast as Demeter. I had been given the role of a grown-up. The performance took place in a modern studio theater. I stood on stage in my black leotard with a red chiffon scarf tied around my waist, and set off. The bright light under which I moved amplified the darkness around it. I had no sense of anyone else being out there, either taking part in the dance or watching. As I became

---

*As Roberto Calasso observes, *Kore* also means the pupil of the eye, and Socrates pointed out that when you look into someone's eyes, it is in their pupils that you might see yourself reflected.

the story, it became my own, that of a girl who was becoming fixed and so went in search of a buried self. Just when it seemed that everything would be as it always had been, the tiniest enactment of desire—six pomegranate seeds!—would render me divided and qualified. When the lights went up I was stuck, still performing, still searching. There may have been a lot of noise coming from me but I could neither hear nor understand. A friend's visit was canceled. My parents were talking as if wrapping me in a blanket. I was hurried home.

# A GROPE PIZZICATO

*I'm a child again when I was really*
*miserable, a grope pizzicato . . .*
—FRANK O'HARA,
"On Rachmaninoff's Birthday"

I wanted other music, the kind I heard in passing from a car, through an open window, from behind the doors of older children's rooms. In our last year without television and before we were each given a transistor radio, I started, as I had with books, with what was to hand. This was the late sixties, a period my mother referred to as "the time your father tried to be swinging." They had acquired a handful of pop records: Bob Dylan's *Nashville Skyline*, Simon and Garfunkel's *Bridge Over Troubled Water*, the Beatles' *Yellow Submarine*, the Moody Blues' *In Search of the Lost Chord*, and the soundtracks to *West Side Story* and *Midnight Cowboy*. I hadn't seen these films and I had no idea who anyone was. I read the titles and listened to the lyrics as if deciphering hieroglyphics. To me, Bob Dylan was another form of music box or wind-up toy. There was a box gramophone in the corner of the living room, and I would crouch over it, put on *Nashville Skyline*, and close my eyes. If I could, I would have dug a foxhole in the floor or put up a tent.

I can't remember my parents playing these records and it never occurred to me that they might do so after I had gone to bed. I assumed that they were my discovery and my secret. My parents had fetched up as medical students in fifties London. She arrived from the Sorbonne, he from National Service. They married in 1958, and two years later, the first of their children was born. My father was starting out in general practice. When would they have time to listen to music? If you don't hear this kind of music at the right time, can it ever make sense to you?

I knew all the words to *Nashville Skyline* long before I knew what they meant: LAY LAY DEE LAY, LAYER PONYA BIG BRA SPED . . . UNTILLA BRAKE ODAYEE . . . LEMMY CEEYER MAIKIM SERMIYUL. I was not interested in who Dylan was or even what he said but in *how* he said it. He had difficulty finding words and then couldn't get them out straight. I imagined them swelling on his tongue and pushing each other out of shape.

"Lay Lady Lay" was, I thought, a song about delay (and I was right). I worked this out partly from the title, LAY LAY DELAY, but also from the feel of it, how Dylan injected delay into the lyrics. His delivery of the phrase "big brass bed" stands rhythmically apart from what is going on around it, which might be why, once I realized what the words were, the image came to stand out so. I wasn't interested in the drama of the man asking a woman to spend the night with him. I was captivated by the emblematic vision of that huge, golden, shining, empty bed.

In the opening duet with Johnny Cash, "Girl from the North Country," I recognized an echo of a song I knew, "Scarborough Fair," yet this was not what I thought of as singing. Dylan and Cash were out there struggling through the snow, barely able to gather the strength to hit the note. Their fraying harmonies are the most moving thing on the record, especially when they lift at the end, becoming freer and higher as they repeat the barely recognizable phrase "true love of mine."

On this album, Dylan is feeling out the big words in particular and letting them go only when the edges have been worn down. For years, I didn't realize that these spasmodic moans were in fact "cruel," "fool," and so on. The words falter, their connections fail in an awkward pause such as "she said she'd always . . . stay" or an odd moment in which the word gets stuck. This left me with the feeling of not having quite caught whatever it was the man was throwing away.

What takes three minutes to play seemed to take ten minutes to listen to. It provoked emotions and suggested circumstances I couldn't wait to experience—being trapped by regret or riveted by desire; trying to be offhand about passion or grown-up about loss; moving on or giving in. It was, for me, a rehearsal of feeling.

A woman who babysat for us remembered me at the age of eight, throwing myself back on a chaise longue and declaring that what I wanted when I grew up was peace in my life. Listening to *Nashville Skyline*, I could be quiet at least: someone else was making my noise for me.

# COME ON SOMETHING

Romeo: *O brawling love . . .*
—WILLIAM SHAKESPEARE,
*Romeo and Juliet,* I:i

I walked down the street apart because I was not in 1960s London but 1950s New York, where people communicated in whistles and finger clicks, where life was not black and white but red and blue, and where conversation tipped over into song, fight into dance, emotion into grace.

*West Side Story* was a fire-engine-red album cover with high-rise black lettering propping up a fire escape on which the sharp silhouettes of a man and woman danced (fell? fought?). From the first whistles and clicks, the spasmic strings and brass, it erupts into a drama of such extension and motion that I gave myself up to it. This music has its own architecture, machinery, circulation, boundaries, and weather. I got lost and found myself back where I started. I passed places I'd seen earlier. I found dead ends, alleys, shocking open spaces, blind corners, and always the pleasurable sense of something building. A city still building itself—what could be more exciting and alive?

And these characters who spat or sang were neither adult nor child. Until I saw the film, they weren't characters at all but each a formulation of feeling. I was astounded that they could be talking, quite ordinarily, *more* than ordinarily, and from there, burst into song. I thought people either stood around talking or stood around singing, but here was a new possibility: you could go about your life and then, when the mood took you, you could dance, you could sing, and everyone around you would know the words and the steps, and just like that the world would be musical.

Here were boys, bristling and strutting and unlike London's floaty hippies, end-of-the-pier Teddy Boys, or prissy Mods, they were completely *boy*. They fought, smoked, and swore even as they sang and danced. The opening scene in which the Jets strut through their territory, threatening and teasing and showing off, is described in the libretto as "half-danced, half-mimed," as if the whole of it lay in movement.

Song and dance are explosion and interruption, and sometimes the only way to keep up with what's happening. Mid-strut, the boys pause, spin, and glide, their arms opening into a port de bras (which means "carriage of the arms," and it was as if they were carrying arms), parting the air as if to reclaim a space they felt themselves losing. They could sing and dance and then get back to business; they could have feelings, and they could recover from them. In the musical world, everything was elastic. People could fly and fall without hurting themselves and they bounced from one scene of their lives to the next, pinging back into shape as they went.

Leonard Bernstein wrote in his *West Side Log* in 1956 (by which time he and Arthur Lorenz had been ruminating on the idea of *West Side Story* for seven years), "Chief problem: to tread the fine line between opera and Broadway, between realism and poetry, ballet and 'just dancing' . . . The line is there, but it's very

fine, and sometimes takes a lot of peering around to discern it."
Like the narrowest tenement, *West Side Story* is built on this fine
line, which is why it is such a volatile structure, why it keeps
falling and rebuilding. The score is kept teetering by the use
throughout of the destabilizing tritone. This is an interval of
three tones, or six semitones, which sounds powerfully unsettled.
So much so that in the Middle Ages it was known as *diabolus in
musica*. It is the augmented fourth, the diminished fifth. Play
middle C and F sharp on the piano and your ear will insist that
something has gone wrong or has been stretched too far.

The Jets and the Sharks meet at a dance in the gym. No
one speaks but everyone dances, through a sequence of
"Blues–Promenade–Mambo–Cha-Cha." These dances are exple-
tive, plosive, headline and subtext. This is war, and even the girls,
who mostly simper and flounce, produce some brutal moves. It
wasn't the girls I identified with, nor was it Tony and Maria, the
simpering Romeo and Juliet. I identified with the music.

The architecture of *West Side Story*, with its use of motif and
reprise, taught me the pleasure of finding something familiar in
an unfamiliar place, differently lit so that it offered some new aspect of itself, another facet, texture, or angle. Here, it was
"Tonight," a song we first hear as Tony and Maria's soppy duet but
which returns as the pivot around which everyone's conflicting in-
terests turn. Tonight there will be a truce, tonight there will be a
battle, tonight there will be an escape, tonight there will be a seduction. Everyone is singing to themselves, but the music pulls
them together like the spokes of a wheel rolling inexorably toward
a final collision as in Homer's ring of dancers or a circle game.

At the end of *West Side Story*, the singing gives way and the im-
petus it provided disappears. No one is able to move forward
from this moment. Perhaps it has something to do with needing
to listen. When you are singing, how can you listen, especially to
yourself? Leonard Bernstein:

At the denouement, the final dramatic unraveling, the music stops and we talk it. Tony is shot and Maria picks up the gun and makes that incredible speech, "How many bullets are left?" My first thought was that this was to be her biggest aria. I can't tell you how many tries I made on that aria. I tried once to make it cynical and swift. Another time like a recitative. Another time like a Puccini aria. In every case, after five or six bars, I gave up. It was phony . . .

# 9

# SPANISH DANCER

*And all at once it is completely fire.*
—RAINER MARIA RILKE,
"Spanish Dancer"

In the photograph, I am turning away from the noise I am making. The tambourine in my right hand is the focus of the picture and I am hiding behind it. My left hand and left leg are blurred. I must have been clapping and stamping my foot.

It is my seventh birthday, summer 1969, and the photograph was taken in Aberbach, Pembrokeshire, Wales. I know that because we went there every summer, and behind the girl in the flamenco dress that landscape progresses through a field of seedy grass and towering gorse to wet green woods and a corner of stone-gray sea.

Aberbach is a green place, green and damp, but I am red-hot, dancing on the mossy stone terrace. My scarlet dress is covered in white polka dots and has white puff sleeves. Its skirt has three flounces fringed with black tassels. I have never had, or wanted, a dress like this. My dresses are simple shifts, nothing more than rectangles. This dress is a kind of reward, or perhaps a reminder. I am a girl. My blond hair is scraped back beneath a clumpy black wig that comes complete with a lace veil I want to call a mantilla, but it is no more than a nylon shiver, a shadow across my face.

The costume fits me perfectly, even the shoes, which I slip on and off like Cinderella unable to believe her luck. They are what delight me most: transparent plastic edged in white ribbon with high heels that change not only my posture but, like some metamorphic device, my shape.

I burn instantly in the sun, and in this picture you can see me burning. My skin is pink, my cheeks red, my mouth crimson. Perhaps I am not turning away from the noise after all but turning into it.

# 10

# VENTAGES

Hamlet: *Will you play upon this pipe?*

Guildenstern: *My Lord, I cannot . . .*

Hamlet: *'Tis as easie as lying. Governe*
*these Ventiges with your finger and thumbe,*
*give it breath with your mouth, and it will*
*discourse most eloquent Musicke . . .*

—WILLIAM SHAKESPEARE,
*Hamlet*, III:iii

W e started with recorders, the practice instrument on which one makes practice music. The sound is that of a rough sketch, of unseasoned breath. We brought our recorders home from school and played, but never together. Only later, once we could read music, were we given instruments of our own and expected to play with other people.

I was allocated the violin. My elder brother played the trombone, my sister the flute, and my little brother the cornet. This child's trumpet suited him. I could see him crossing a battlefield protected by his perpetual jeunesse, his air of being exempt and elsewhere. The cornet depended upon a subtle control of breath that I could never have been expected to master. My brother, though, suited the restraint and complexity of the instrument, and in relation to him I think of it not as flaring open but tapering back toward the mouth—a reverse megaphone for someone who knows that to speak quietly is to be heard loudly.

I once took my sister's flute from her hands but could not make a noise. She, of course, had the instrument that looked like a wand. It suited her combination of steeliness and modesty, her air of knowing more than she was saying and of being capable of more than one might expect. I led our adventures but depended on her to realize them. I went first over the wall or up the tree but she had to help me up and then manage by herself.

Both cornet and flute concern the angle and strength of breath, and the Little Ones, as they were known, were more subtle than us older two. My big brother's trombone was all comic potential and swagger. It evolved from the sackbut, the name of which derives from Old French: *sacquer* and *bouter*—to push and to pull. This was my brother—granting the rest of us an audience, the chance to participate in his world, and then dropping us with a shrug and a smile.

I cannot remember the sound I made on the violin and I did not enjoy trying to play it, but I liked to hold and carry it. The weight of the case in my hand felt just right—significant but not onerous. The case itself was pleasing with its flaking black exterior and sumptuous trashy crushed-velvet lining. I enjoyed greasing the bow with rosin, stuff that was sticky and dry at the same time, and marveled that the bow was horsehair—I had never seen any such hair on a horse.

Playing the violin hurt. I had to clench it between my left shoulder and chin, and my right arm had to keep the bow lifted. When I read the story of Orpheus and how his lyre was grafted to his body, I thought a lyre must be like a violin. Your own arm disappears and is replaced by the instrument, which is grafted to your collarbone and chin. In keeping with any curse, you cannot speak, you cannot move, you can only play. Recently, I was watching a chamber orchestra and thought that more so than with any other instrument, the violin becomes part of the body. Good musicians are physically dissolved when playing, and for violinists, who cannot see where to place their fingers and have nothing to guide them through touch, music must be more than ever about memory rather than fingertips and breath; the ventage is deeper, more of the self, closer to singing.

With this instrument I had to imagine making music. I found it hard enough to learn how to sense where a note would be, let alone to give it any character. The sounds I produced were those of physical failure: my pizzicato notes were as raw as my fingertips, and my bowed notes as thin and shaky as my arms. Instead of making music, I was struggling to manage an instrument. It seemed so sensitive and conditional that I began to understand how notes took shape and how little their shape had to do with dots on a stave. I was beginning to learn this about language, too.

# 11

# WHAT SHALL I DO TO
# BE SAVED?

*The way to heaven is too steep, too narrow, for men
to dance in and keep revel rout. No way is large or
smooth enough for capering rousters, for jumping,
skipping, dancing dames but that broad, beaten,
pleasant road that leads to HELL.*

—WILLIAM PRYNNE,
*Histriomastix*

To be a teenager in 1970 was to suffer an excess of gravity. I watched them move slowly along Camden High Street, boys and girls alike with faces half-closed behind long, center-parted hair. The shape their clothes made was that of something being pulled down into the earth: scoop-necked tops, pear-drop collars, flared or leg-of-mutton sleeves, and flared ankle-length skirts and trousers made of cumbersome corduroy, denim, or hessian. They wore bare feet or sandals in summer and otherwise heavy boots or wedge-platform shoes. In winter they wrapped up in afghans, antique fur coats and greatcoats, hats and scarves. Their colors were vegetal—umber, ocher, aubergine, mushroom, sage. They looked damp.

I thought that their music must be the key to becoming like them. I got to know it as we absorb music in passing but can remember only its seriousness and weight. The record sleeves had the same droopy, glutinous lettering as the clothes-shop signs. The music of lumbering lost creatures. Is that what I had to become?

There was a higher realm, occupied by beautiful men who might be women, who wore feather boas and silver eye shadow, their hair in ringlets, solid wedges, and angular curtains, and who seemed remote, gentle, and dangerous. If the Camden hippie colors were earthbound, the glam-rock colors were like the whirl of gas around a planet. I glimpsed these figures passing in and out of adult doorways, their paths through the city crossing mine as indifferently as if we were in separate orbits. So much about them was concentrated in their surfaces that they seemed weightless. They suggested a perfection that I would have to move through many worlds in order to attain.

They looked like David Bowie on the cover of *Ziggy Stardust*. He poses on a narrow pavement strewn with rubbish in a city of gas lamps and cardboard boxes. It is dark and raining. The buildings are soggy brown, the sky gray, the huddle of parked cars black, gray, and white. Bowie has silver-green-blond hair, silver-green skin, and is wearing a jumpsuit that looks like a spacesuit.

Such creatures were neither bad nor good—they were other. They complicated my idea of beauty and persuaded me to submit to much that I didn't understand. Their songs might as well have been written in another language, but they were delivered with such conviction and style that they too were a triumph of surface.

There was a great deal of music-making, and a feeling that

anyone could and should do it. A lot of people carried guitars and would sit down and play wherever they were—on a patch of grass, at a bus stop, at any kind of gathering. A group of local musicians had set up a Saturday-morning music school for children, and I played the violin in the orchestra and sang in the choir. That year, the Young Music Makers staged a production of *The Pilgrim's Progress* at the nearby Roundhouse, a vast circular building I knew well, but only from the outside. I had never imagined a way into it.

The Roundhouse was one of my childhood's architectural features, like the Mermaid Theatre or the Post Office Tower. I took such names literally and had the notion that in the darkness of the theatre our legs turned into fishtails, that letters were sorted twenty floors up, and that the Roundhouse was someone's house, only round. Then I was told that it was a place where the Victorians had repaired steam engines, and I wondered how they got the train in—perhaps coiled like a snake. This information convinced me that the Roundhouse must be even bigger than it looked. Even so, steam engines had apparently become too large for it and, for the next hundred years, the Roundhouse had been used to store thousands of bottles of whiskey and gin. So the train uncoiled itself, the steam evaporated, and that vast space filled up with row upon row of glistening bottles. Not in boxes, of course, but lined up as they would be behind the bar in a Western, reflected in mirrors, only in the Roundhouse there would be no mirrors but more and more actual bottles wherever you looked. I wondered how anyone could walk among them without knocking one and what would happen if one fell. Would it be like dominoes, bottle after bottle crashing down till Camden was awash with alcohol and glass?

The trains and the gin were long gone, and by 1970, the Roundhouse had become a rock venue. I saw the posters: David Bowie, Marc Bolan, Jimi Hendrix, Pink Floyd, the Rolling Stones, the Doors, and the Who, names that were for me part of the musical ether through which teenagers moved. This featureless, squat building was now a fairy-tale castle.

Now I was to enter the castle. Of course it was not as large as I had known it to be and the bare brick walls said nothing of trains or gin or Jimi Hendrix. I listened to someone explain that here in the center there had been a vast turning circle on which to move the engines, and my train uncoupled and diminished to a squat front end. In order to change into our black-and-white pilgrim attire we were taken down into the undercroft, the rings of tunnels and corridors beneath the turning-circle floor. I was so transfixed by the undercroft that I remember nothing of the performance. I was not touched by the music, or by the story of the pilgrim, and I had found no trace of the building's other musical life, no clue, no key. I recently asked my brother. "All I remember," he said, "is running around in those tunnels."

Would I really one day be released onto the broad, beaten, and pleasant road of Camden High Street? Would I learn to move slowly or would it just occur, this arrival of gravity? I could neither ask these questions nor answer them. All I could do was keep running around and around in my eight-year-old orbit until the turning circle moved like some cosmic pivot and I was tipped into another orbit and a heavier atmosphere.

# 12

# COVER VERSIONS

Oberon: *And this Ditty, after me,*
*Sing, and dance it trippinglie.*

Titania: *First, rehearse this song by roate:*
*To each word a warbling note . . .*

—WILLIAM SHAKESPEARE,
*A Midsummer Night's Dream*, V:i

L ondon was still dark. There were blanks and bomb sites
and cratered backstreets where the lights that went out
with the war had not yet gone back on. The Houses of
Parliament were shabby with centuries of soot. Most people
dressed quietly and sensibly. At school we watched chalk on
blackboard, and at home, black-and-white television.

My mother's cooking was half Mrs. Beeton, half New Age—
roast beef, kedgeree, steak-and-kidney pudding, liver and bacon,
but also boiled wheat and ratatouille with a salad of dandelion
leaves yanked out of the lawn. There was something called Gurd-
jieff Salad—a purple foment of beetroot, tomatoes, apples, and
red peppers. Our bread was dense brown bricks made by my
mother, who was indulgent enough to supply sliced white bread

as well. When we came home from school, tea was on the table. It consisted of anything from chopped raw cabbage and sliced oranges to pork pie and chocolate cake. The cake would be homemade on an industrial scale and served up in slabs from a roasting dish. My mother then prepared our main meal for when my father got back from evening surgery at eight. She made three or four meals a day for at least six and often ten or more people, and always provided dessert (rhubarb crumble, Eve's pudding, zabaglione, apple snow), yet she did not like gadgets. She had a Kenwood mixer, which could take on anything, but we had neither toaster nor electric kettle. She saved time by grilling bread on one side only and conditioning us not to want to drink anything with our meals.

School lunches combined black and white with Technicolor. Gray slices of beef, darker gray cabbage, and lighter gray roast potatoes sat next to jade-bright peas, bullion-yellow fish fingers, and mailbox-red baked beans. Dessert was a glassful of straw-berry-pink foam with a cherry-colored glacé cherry on top, or leathery jelly that looked so green it convinced me that it tasted of lime. There was also sponge pudding or tart served with cus-tard. The tart tasted dry and the custard wet but they were prop-erly pink and yellow. Even the milk in the custard seemed artificial, its texture that of something whose molecules had been rearranged. No one worried about additives. My eyes itched, my stomach bloated, my lips swelled, and I felt some afternoons as if I'd been clubbed, yet I craved this stuff. Often, the pink foam or lime jelly would be all I ate.

Occasionally shop-bought confections appeared on the table at home: Swiss Rolls and Wagon Wheels. When we turned up our noses at a cake she'd bought because it was cut-price and past its sell-by date, my mother noted the sugar content, made a calcula-tion, melted it down, and greeted us the next afternoon with a plate of fudge, which we devoured. ("It was the doily that did it," she later observed.) Now and then she would offer us Angel Delight, which we could make ourselves by whisking a sachet of powder into a pint of milk and leaving it to set for one minute. We stood in a row by the fridge door and counted down.

Artificial colors and flavors suggested the heightened and simplified world of the cartoon, in which everything has become a simulacrum—not so much an image of itself as an image of that image. I didn't buy my first real record until 1972 but, for a year or so, rehearsed the act by buying *Top of the Pops* albums, cover versions of recent hits. Like artificial colors and flavors, these versions were more themselves than themselves. With their coloring-book definition and lack of depth, they were easy for a child to make sense of: strawberry mousse.

Like someone looking at Dürer's rhinoceros four hundred years ago, I knew this was not the real thing but I didn't yet understand why that mattered. I was not ready for real taste or texture.

There was another kind of cover version, as *Top of the Pops* also featured the dance troupe Pan's People. Each week they gave a recent hit single a heavily themed interpretation. They might be wartime sweethearts, teachers, or astronauts and simply rearranged or embellished the same old moves accordingly. This was the world of the fairy king and queen, where everything could be rearranged as everything else, the mechanical fantastic where everything was plastic and everything was play.

And what of my mother? It was only many years later when I heard someone ask her why she had never practiced as a doctor that this question occurred to me. Her reasons are her own but they include the fact that having been brought up by nannies, she wanted to look after her children herself. She protected us from expectation and we grew up vague in our ambitions while gradually discovering what we were for. The complicated model I was given was no cover version. It made a complicated life seem possible.

# 13

# CRUSH

*Vronsky was a dark, squarely built man of medium
height, with an exceptionally tranquil and firm
expression on his good-natured, handsome face.
Everything about his head and figure, from the
closely cropped black hair and freshly shaven chin
to the loosely fitting, brand-new uniform, was simple and at the same time elegant.*

—LEO TOLSTOY,
*Anna Karenina*

As I came to understand music as social currency, I realized that I needed to declare an allegiance. One day, I
was watching television and saw the one for me. Donny
Osmond was intriguingly poised between good boy and bad. His
face was still chubby and his hair had been brushed firmly into
place. On the other hand, it had been allowed to grow long
enough to suggest trouble—the length at which my brother's
headmaster demanded hair be cut. He wore jeans. They looked
pressed. He wore a cap, which was fashionable. It reminded me
of the one my father wore to go sailing.

He was wholesome, but in that pumped-up American way which dazzled us then. His teeth and eyes were shiny, and as he loafed around a playground singing in his high, brash voice, he sat down on a swing and sighed and suddenly looked capable of complication. He was singing about "puppy love" but he was being ironic, and I was pleased to have understood that. The lyrics were basic, really just a net for the force of the arrangement behind him—instead of the chirpy economies of bubblegum pop, here was what sounded like several orchestras' worth of violinists, grand pianos, choruses, and harps adding up to a surge of generalized emotion.

I was impressed by such grandeur, and felt it matched the scale of the unformed feelings for which I badly needed an object. I had a crush on a boy at school, and I looked at Donny Osmond and decided, quite consciously, that he would be my favorite pop star. Somehow I knew I needed one, and as I'd never heard of him, I assumed no one else had either. I was looking for my first musical discovery and wanted it to be as private and singular as my feelings about the boy at school. One thing I grasped from the start was the cachet of obscurity. I told no one about the boy and no one about Donny. The next day someone mentioned Donny's name and I dropped him. I turned ten and "Puppy Love" was Number One.

There was another American boy—David Cassidy. He was older, more complicated, more fashionable, and the star of a television series called *The Partridge Family*. These American boys were feminine and masculine in ways that did not ironize each other. Like the Spartans Herodotus describes combing their long hair before the battle of Thermopylae, these boys clearly knew how to handle a blow-dryer as well as a fight. But while I thought of those soldiers as being carved out of marble and bronze, the Americans looked as if they'd been made out of generic Boy Stuff, something bland and malleable, set in a regular mold.

Their superbeauty was a triumph of proportion and symmetry. It impressed but it did not disturb, and for a few months this was what I needed, the idea of Boy in its most benign and consistent form.

I assumed that the boys I knew would become like the men I knew—silent and bearded or silent and lipsticked. These cheery, sensitive Americans, who would in actuality remain thousands of miles and an ocean away, were a safer place to start.

# 14

# TAXONOMY

*Tune thy Music to thy heart . . .*
—THOMAS CAMPION

In 1972, I bought my first single and began to study the charts. I lost sight of Donny Osmond and David Cassidy immediately. The single was Chicory Tip's "Son of My Father," stomping and repetitive but made strange by the swirls and wails of a Moog synthesizer, a ghost caught in a machine.

I was starting to see pop in terms of style and structure, and *Top of the Pops* was my map. I knew all those teenagers crowding around the presenter and the bands were real. They looked it—awkward, smirking, dancing as if they'd never heard music before. I began to understand pop as a construction. This was not a spontaneous party scene. These people had applied, had queued, and were now being herded and prompted through the evening (which was probably not evening at all). Marooned among them were bands I was beginning to classify. Like a child filling a stamp album or collecting eggs, I needed to create order and name names.

*Nursery*
Melanie—"Brand New Key"
The New Seekers—"I'd Like to Teach the World to Sing"
Wings—"Mary Had a Little Lamb"
The Royal Scots Dragoon Guards Band —"Little Drummer
   Boy"

*Playground*
Benny Hill—"Ernie, the Fastest Milkman in the West"
Chuck Berry—"My Ding-a-Ling"

*Vitamins*
Michael Jackson—"Rockin' Robin"
Little Eva—"The Loco-Motion"

*Sulk*
Alice Cooper—"School's Out"
T. Rex—"Children of the Revolution"
Slade—"Mama Weer All Crazee Now"
Mott the Hoople—"All the Young Dudes"

*Smirk*
Hot Butter—"Popcorn"
Lieutenant Pigeon—"Mouldy Old Dough"

*Sweets*
Lynsey de Paul—"Sugar Me"
The Supremes—"Automatically Sunshine"

*Oompah*
Jimmy Osmond—"Long-Haired Lover from Liverpool"
Jeff Beck—"Hi-Ho Silver Lining"

*Motorbike*
Gary Glitter—"Rock 'n' Roll Parts I & II"
The Shangri-Las—"Leader of the Pack"

*Squirm*
Love Unlimited—"Walkin' in the Rain with the One I Love"
Roberta Flack—"The First Time Ever I Saw Your Face"

*Who?*
Don McLean—"Vincent"
Roxy Music—"Virginia Plain"
David Bowie—"The Jean Genie"
Bread—"Guitar Man"
Elton John—"Rocket Man"
T. Rex—"Metal Guru"
10cc—"Donna"

*?*
Procol Harum—"A Whiter Shade of Pale"
Diana Ross—"Doobeedoo 'Ndoobe Doobeedoo 'Ndoobe
     Doobeedoo 'Ndoo"
Gilbert O'Sullivan—"Ooh-Wakka-Doo-Wakka-Day"
The Moody Blues—"Nights in White Satin"

What was a light fandango? Who was Vincent? Who was the Guitar Man, the Star Man, the Rocket Man, the Jean Genie, Virginia Plain, Donna, the Metal Guru?

All these were in the charts in 1972. Some I associate with being six and some with being sixteen. I suppose at ten I was something of both.

# 15

# LAUGHING GAS

*As I was on the road, observing the littleness of the houses, the trees, the cattle and the people, I began to think myself in Lilliput. I was afraid of trampling on every traveller I met, and often called aloud to have them stand out of the way, so I had like to have gotten one or two broken heads for my impertinence.*

—JONATHAN SWIFT,
*Gulliver's Travels*

Art: Lavinia shows interest and works in a very personal style—this tends to be rather messy.

We left London in January 1973, no one now seems to remember why, and moved thirty-five miles northeast to an Essex village. The world both opened up and contracted as the city gave way to bare flat fields and a view that was mostly sky, while the lights went out. I had not known true countryside darkness, and that winter, power cuts meant that our evenings were lived by oil lamp. Low cottages huddled together and people doubled over in the face of the eastern wind that was said to blow in straight from Siberia. The waiting of childhood, the waiting to be told what was happening, was replaced by waiting for something to happen—the arrival of a bus, the appearance of a friend.

Form tutor: Carelessness and indiscipline bedevil this report . . . Lavinia tends to be very extreme emotionally . . . I think she needs to give herself more time for everything.

That September I started secondary school. It was a new school injected into the grounds of a failing secondary modern, an "Anglo-European" school in a brief era of European fervor. Until then, there had only been the Continent—a place of palaces but not many kings and queens, where everyone spoke several languages, trains ran on time, teenagers shook hands, and people left bicycles unlocked. Cars started and houses were warm. (A woman I knew, who came to London from Berlin in the thirties, was appalled by the damp and chill and declared, "Even the Romans had central heating!") The Continent was also dangerous. It harbored rabies and revolution, and you couldn't drink the water.

Geography: She does not exert herself to present ideas and facts in an ordered manner.

Europe, on the other hand, was the land of butter mountains, wine lakes, and a forest of red tape. It was

Europe's fault that we had to eat French apples and that farmers were planting rape, whose acid-yellow flowers clashed with the poppies and made everyone sneeze. Europe was regulated, corporate, and bland. You could drink the water, but you wouldn't have much fun.

It now seems odd that a school established in order to celebrate European unity asserted the distinction between island and mainland in its name, as if our relationship was at best hyphenated. I knew more about Walter Gropius than I did about Turner, and more about Valéry Giscard d'Estaing than Cromwell, but although I learned French, German, and Russian, I had about as much opportunity to speak them as I would have Ancient Greek, so they faded.

Only we, the first year, had to wear the new uniform, which took its colors from the European Community flag. All summer I looked forward to this azure-and-gold future only to be issued with a puff-sleeved banana-yellow shirt and a royal-blue Crimplene jacket and skirt. We were also supposed to wear a lapel badge with the flag's ring of gold stars, as if we were delegates to some interminable conference.

Art: Lavinia has not followed instructions precisely this term. She must make some effort to conform at this early stage or else the basic building methods will escape her.

The scale and speed of life changed as the world grew smaller and slower, and the horizon emptier.

Nothing that had worked before worked now. I had to learn a new geography and also a new way of measuring it. Some years earlier, decimalization had meant relearning money, and around the time I started this new school, we had to switch from imperial to metric measurement. I could do the sums but I developed no sense of meters or kilograms.

Chemistry: Lavinia has a negative attitude toward science and has made some progress as a result of her intelligence and not by design.

I didn't work: my language, accent, codes, and clothes were all wrong. People laughed at my name and mimicked the way I spoke. My voice was too posh, I had ink on my shirt, I was messy and skinny and dead white.

German: She needs to realize that the oral aspect of any language is of paramount importance.

Perhaps out of a desire to bypass my age, perhaps because I was so bad at being a child, I related to older girls, and if one spoke kindly to me, would follow her around until she shouted at me to go away. I had no idea of myself and no idea of what I was doing. I was taken to a new ballet class, a new violin teacher, but it was as if they were teaching a different kind of music.

I looked into mirrors but only ever at my face,

where I saw my thin skin already worn through and
exposing what it contained, which surged and then
settled under my eyes. I tried restoring my skin with
my mother's makeup but this drew attention from
other older girls, the ones who had noticed my odd-
ity and nervousness and who then, for a year or so,
made me into a game.

English: Lavinia
writes as fluently
as ever, but I
would prefer her
to do so less
impulsively. A
more controlled
and disciplined
style should now
be emerging.

I was usually bewildered, and often terrified. The
world, which had begun to fall into place, unan-
chored and distorted. I, too, shrank and veered, and
felt in any given situation that I was wrong—standing
in the wrong place and making the wrong shapes, the
wrong noise. At primary school, if people weren't
your friend they ignored you but here they pursued
you and told you what you looked like and who you
were. I wasn't ready for that so retreated further into
my body by convincing myself I was ill. I also became
abruptly nearsighted and, as chalk floated off black-
boards and people's faces were wiped out, was re-
lieved to stop trying to see.

German: At other
times, she
"switches off."

That winter, the Parent-Teacher Association gave a
dance in the school hall. My parents came, and like a
child before the invention of the teenager, I dressed

like my mother. There was music for grown-ups and
music for children. The song that was most in-
escapable at that time was David Bowie's "Laughing
Gnome," a brittle piece of nonsense to which people
sang along in the same helium way—"Ha ha ha, hee
hee hee . . ." Its mindless tempo, its pert lyrics,
Bowie's voice thinned to a nasal malevolence—this
was strained music in every sense.

A friend of my elder brother's took me for a walk
around the school grounds, sat me down on a bench
under a willow tree, and gave me my first kiss.

English: My one
appeal is always
for discipline!
and beware over-
sentimentality too,
Lavinia!

For months afterward I daydreamed about him and
waited for what would happen next. Nothing did. In
the move, I had managed to get the old box gramophone for myself, and I would shut myself away in my
room for hours, playing the handful of records I had,
imagining the boy finding me there. That is how I
wanted him to see me, listening to music. We wouldn't
have to talk because we'd be listening to music.

At the end of the first year, we went on a school
trip to Brittany. The class mocked but tolerated me,
and the teachers seemed to take the same approach.
I woke one day with toothache so severe I could not
speak and stayed on my camp bed in the dormitory.
One teacher decided I was making a fuss about nothing, and every now and then someone, I remember
most clearly a boy who had seemed so kind, would
come into the dormitory to say something contemp-

tuous. There was a needle in my jaw, and these needling voices were pushing it deeper.

On the last night, the teacher allowed a "disco." There were thirty twelve-year-olds (only I was not twelve yet), a handful of records, and a microphone in the dining hall, under striplights. They played another novelty record, "The Streak," which was rude and trite enough to have become a playground song. As the others milled around in hectic imitation, I ignored the pain in my jaw and yelled the words. It was as if I were shouting at them to let me in.

As the pain grew larger, I grew smaller and everyone else drifted farther away. When I got home, I was taken to the dentist, who found an abscess beneath a milk tooth so rotten that it more or less fell out.

I looked around, took note, and changed. I was a small person in a small place. I developed a small voice and a small laugh—*ha ha ha, hee hee hee.* The adult tooth didn't come through for years, and when it did was less like enamel than eggshell.

# 16

# I LATE WENT SINGING

*"Once I was sitting in the little kitchen of the Three Choughs at Casterbridge, having a bit of dinner, and a brass band struck up in the street. Sich a beautiful band as that were! I was sitting eating fried liver and lights, I well can mind—ah, I was! and to save my life, I couldn't help chawing to the tune. Band played six-eight time; six-eight chaws I, willynilly. Band plays common; common time went my teeth among the fried liver and lights as true as a hair."*

—THOMAS HARDY,
*Under the Greenwood Tree*

The background sounds of the village were percussive: church bells, the cawing of rooks, and the swish and rumble of traffic. Above that ran the airy noise of children whose shouts, threats, pleas, and games simplified on the wind into bleats and swoops. Adult noise was either the careful building of greetings and transactions, or mutters and sighs like those a house releases as it tries to settle.

I lived in that village between the ages of eleven and eighteen, when I was neither a child nor a grown-up and so while I
listened, I would not join in. Sometimes adults burst into song.
This happened in the pub or in church, but also in my home,
where our large, empty living room became a kind of second village hall. I would be making coffee for friends in the kitchen
when the house would fill with "Swanee! How I love ya, how I
love ya, my dear old Swanee!"

"What the fuck is that?"

"What?"

"That . . . *singing*."

"No idea."

"But it's coming from your living room."

"Is it?"

"And it sounds racist."

"It's not racist. It's some sort of barbershop thing."

"Barber what? Why are they doing it in your house?"

"It's nothing to do with me. Let's go upstairs."

It was something to do with me because it was my father, the
village doctor, along with the dentist, lawyer, and bank manager,
*singing*. They did it well and it sounded convincing but, at thirteen, I was mortified. By that age, my singing had been reduced
to singing along to records in my bedroom. The shrieking of a
gaggle of girls walking down the street might tip over into some
blurted lyrics, but this was done to entertain one another and to
resist the decorous volume at which life was going on around us.
We mimed in assembly and refused to join the choir. We didn't
do the kind of singing that meant *joining in*.

We required our grown-ups to be grown-ups and so found it
unsettling when they dressed up, danced, or sang. Still climbing
out of childhood, we needed to see the seriousness of what was
ahead of us, to make a distinction. The doctor in blackface and a
boater? When the police stopped him for speeding on the way

home from the performance, he hadn't even bothered to take his makeup off.


My father had a friend called Raymond, who was an opera singer. A Yorkshireman, he was bluff and warm, and liked to tell stories about his days in the chorus at Covent Garden when careful timing enabled him to nip out during a performance for a pint in the pub next door. We were fond of Raymond. He lived with his wife in Surrey, or at least I think he did, as he seemed to be perpetually on the road.

For some years, he turned up at our house each week and gave singing lessons, and so we would come home from school to hear the women of the village going through their arpeggios and scales. There was something unbearable about hearing them struggle to make a real noise. We expected strength from our grown-ups, and would rather have them confidently burst into song than display such querulousness. It reminded me of the way women who enter a room late sometimes creep as if doubled up by shame, and there is something shameful about that.

Their noise was not loud but it carried. We hurried through our tea and biscuits, and went to turn on a radio or the television, to shut doors and pull pillows over our heads because it was like having a bird trapped in the chimney. Wherever you went in the house, you could hear this tremulous flutter: "a aa A *AA* A aa aah . . . a aa A *AA* A aa aah . . . a aa A *AA* A aa aah . . . a aa A *AA* A aa aah . . . a aa A *AA* A aa aah . . ."

If there were a sound that something makes when it gets on your nerves, then this would be it. I wonder now if it was those arpeggios that kept Raymond on the move up and down the country—a flock of birds too timid to fly, flapping along in his wake: "a aa A *AA* A aa aah . . ."

\* \* \*

Music was the only thing that filled that living room. My mother's madrigal choir met there for a while, and I remember them standing around congenially, as if huddled on a church path waiting for a newly married couple to appear. Then someone would raise a hand and they would start to sing, filling the room with a noise that billowed and folded as if tidying itself away. They might have been folding laundry.

The English are keen on the madrigal, a relatively modest form adapted from the Italian, like the sonnet and at around the same time. It has survived from the last Elizabethan age to this, and has about it a complicated stoicism: "Of joys and pleasing pains, I late went singing." I liked these songs for their melancholy but they had a neatness I found unsettling. They were so carefully arranged, their dark corners so well swept; no heart could be broken by a song like that.

The choir carefully completed each sound and each song. They looked the same at the end as they had when they started, and softly departed, helping one another back into their coats, buttoning up and checking their flashlights before setting off home.

At Whitsun, Morris Men would appear outside the pub on the green. I never saw them arrive or leave or *become*, and can only picture them now midleap, those portly, silvering red-faced chaps who smiled as if their smiles were what got them off the ground. They wore flimsy white trousers and shirts, red ribbons around their elbows and knees, and sometimes a waistcoat or sash. They waved sticks and handkerchiefs, and clinked with tiny bells. Someone played a concertina, and that is what the music sounded like—squeezed out. It was effortful and repetitive, and punctuated by the clack of their sticks and the trivial smash of bells as they stamped their feet. It seemed joyless to me.

Morris dancing is hundreds of years old and no one seems to be sure of what it means or where it came from. No wonder it sounds and looks like something that has gotten stuck. Anyone making their way across the green on a Whitsun afternoon would get stuck too. Walking past, I wandered into its tempo and found myself unable to move. This stuck music would be an augury of the leaden summer to come, when I would be here with my family or away with my family, and nothing would happen until September.

Teams of carol singers began to arrive in mid-December. They were raising money for the victims of famine, a new church spire, or the football team's kit; to send deprived children to a farm, or pensioners to the seaside. They were good and bad, sometimes twenty-strong and sometimes just a couple of teenagers who forgot the words and held out an unlabeled tin. They all came to our house because we lived in the middle of the village, and while we children liked to turn off the lights and hide, our parents would throw the door open, join in, give them all something, and more often than not pass around mulled wine and mince pies.

On Christmas Eve, the pubs emptied just as the last bus got in from town and the villagers made for Midnight Mass. My father attended the Protestant church, which was sunlit and hearty and had a gourmet vicar who was keen on ceremony. It was a more professional operation than the Catholic church my mother had adopted. Gloomy and marooned, this was a squat building set back from the road alone with its graveyard, which was walled in by poplars.

For the village to be out and about at midnight was a remarkable thing, and it prompted a kind of all-round benevolence. At the Catholic church, drunks wandered the aisle, tramps were given a seat somewhere warm, and no one laughed at Judge Smallbone's organ playing, even though he might play the previous hymn again or something else altogether. I was happy to join in and sing, and only withdrew back into my teenage self when it came to "making the sign of peace," when I chose to preempt any hugs with a handshake.

In the seventies, the English countryside was half feudal, half looking to the future. Men touched their caps as the squire went by while farmers sold land to property developers. My father cured warts by touching them with a gold watch but he also kept ampoules of diamorphine in a locked cupboard at home. There was less nostalgia than there is now, and more evident history.

The village was not the silent place it seemed, or that I perhaps wanted it to be. From when I arrived I saw it as a place to get out of, and tripped over myself in the rush to grow up and leave. I did not like to think that it had any effect on me, but I was caught up in its rhythms and could not escape its music.

The quietest day of the year was Armistice Sunday. I was usually still asleep as the parade approached the war memorial outside my window. Each year the men were fewer and those left had grown smaller. It was always cold and gray, and while I knew they must be wearing their medals on their black buttoned-up coats, I could not make them out. The same man played a shaky trumpet voluntary each year but the sound I remember is the drum to which they marched—the slow, strong beat of something you wish would pass or wish had never come to pass, and that was caught in its moment and so could not move on or go away.

# 17

# DELICATISSIMAMENTE

*There's slow and there's the discovery of slow.*
*The last bus has not gone, it never comes.*

—"Essex Rag"

I played the piano because it was there and because otherwise time would not pass. I played everything as loudly as I could, foot hard down on the sustain pedal as if driving foot to the floor out of that Essex village. From twelve to eighteen I played most days. While I grasped the mood of the composer's instructions, it did not occur to me that they were being particularly specific about tempo. I played as fast as I could and as slow as I could, and got bored with what lay in between. On later hearing recitals and recordings I barely recognized the sonatas, preludes, and nocturnes I had attempted. My first idea of them was drawn from their atmosphere and character as read rather than listened to. Perhaps I thought of them as novels or poems, a form of resonance to be mapped onto my own coordinates.

My parents found a piano teacher who started me on the music of my jewelry box. "Für Elise," and I played it with that box's plastic ballerina in mind—a jerky twirl followed by an abrupt collapse and a gradual clamber back onto her feet. I asked the teacher for something grown-up and she gave me a simplified version of "Ode to Joy." This I interpreted as no more heartfelt than my music-box "Für Elise." Had I heard the unbowdlerized work, would I have recognized the emotion?

Where would I go to experience joy? I was too young to go to town in the evenings, eight miles away by a bus that came hourly during the day, two-hourly at evenings and weekends if it turned up at all. The reflexive ecstasies of childhood were gone and the adult pursuit of delight was beyond reach. I was stuck in march time, pounding out surplus energy.

The teacher proposed a pop song and got me the sheet music for the Rubettes' "Sugar Baby Love." The piano arrangement was like a pneumatic drill, each chord repeated three times, underlining everything. I had seen the band on *Top of the Pops*—old men in white suits and caps, a falsetto wail followed by a series of feeble apologies: "I didn't mean to make you cry. Oo oo ooo . . ." They wouldn't make me cry; no one could these days.

So this was what it meant to be an arrangement. You took the most adaptable parts, and strengthened and simplified them so that you had an obvious structure. People would like it because they got it. They knew what they were dealing with. It seemed like a good idea to make myself into an arrangement as soon as I could.

The last piece the teacher gave me was Mozart's Piano Sonata in C (K279), encouraging me with the fact that the composer had stipulated that it was for beginners. I had little idea of Mozart, who wrote this when he himself was a teenager. I had been taught something of musical structure—exposition, transition, development, recapitulation—but now I was discovering through my fingers how it added up. I discovered its drama, too: approach, adaptation, complication, retreat.

I loved the way the first movement rushed about, how trilling scales collided with arpeggios that bounced from one hand to the other, and how the left hand overtook the right, which then insisted on its presence in odd phrases and trills. It was like juggling or pinball, a sport I could be good at on my own.

I went on to play the Sonata in D (K284). Its opening movement is flighty, full of things being picked up and dropped. The second movement, a "Rondeau en Polonaise" feels like Mozart in fancy dress. In the sheet-music notes Aubyn Raymar makes a plea for decorum: "That stateliness of manner which belongs to the courtly associations of the dance will not endure inelegant hustle."

The "Allegretto with twelve variations" was beyond me. As Raymar says, most of this movement is

devoted to a provocation of the executant to adroitness in managing different problems of virtuosity. The flowing triplet, continuous semiquaver, legato thirds and octaves in one hand, crossing of hands, tremolo, mordent and trill, are all copiously represented.

Although I could not play it, I was curious enough to read the notes. In the final variation, Raymar draws attention to the rhythm of the closing bars—DUM de de DUM de de, a tumbling meter (as opposed to the limping opposite, de de DUM). This fascinated me—that things could be built out of surprising angles and could finish so openly. I had not expected Mozart to surprise.

Listening to Mozart, I would hear something finished. Trying to play a sonata, I sensed something being made. I wanted to know this one piece of music fully, and even though I had stopped having lessons, corrected my fingering, my use of the pedals, and practiced each passage over and over. I didn't need the music but could not play without it in front of me. I did not

read it or think about it, in fact I could play only if I were thinking about something else. It was as if I had to let my body get on
with it.

I moved from Mozart to Beethoven, starting with what I
thought I knew—the "Moonlight" Sonata. Donald Francis Tovey,
who wrote the notes this time, was adamant: "Moonlight can certainly be very beautiful . . . But moonlight will not suffice to illu-
minate the whole of this sonata . . ."

That first movement is Adagio sostenuto with a note: "Si deve
suonare tutto questo pezzo delicatissimamente e senza sordini."* 
The only word I understood was the hardest to negotiate, hardest to spell, pronounce, even to look at: *delicatissimamente.* Just
how delicate could anyone be? I imagined a pianist shrinking
into a little knot of niceness and timidity. Tovey cuts to the chase:
"How are we to attain a sensitive *pianissimo* that is neither patchy
nor dull?" He goes on to emphasize strength and accent, and
compares the cumulative effect of this movement's endless
triplets—DUM-DUM-DUM DUM-DUM-DUM—to Wordsworth's
lines

> *Rolled round in earth's diurnal course*
> *With rocks, and stones, and trees.*

In other words, the moonlight was also a cement mixer, which
made sense when I thought about the lunar effects on the tides
and the tides' effects on a stony beach.

Tovey invokes Liszt's famous interpretation of the Sonata as a
lesson in the importance of technique, adding, "Beethoven gives
us very little apparatus for working such miracles. Suggestion
plays a large part in them . . ." So much of music is about sugges-

---

*"You must play all of this piece very delicately and on the sly." "On the sly" means without
dampers, that is, with free use of the right pedal.

tion, including the suggestiveness of the player's interpretation, how she has to evoke but not explain so that the listener will lean toward her.

At fifteen, I wanted slow. I no longer ran spontaneously, in fact I was not remotely spontaneous but extremely wary. I liked sad poems and sad songs, and anything moody. My relation to the tempo of the world around me was like that of a record being played at the wrong speed. I found slow most pleasingly in the Adagio movement of the Pathétique Sonata, which I thought I could handle. The only problem was working my way toward it, as ten bars into the first movement, my playing was buried by an extraordinary chromatic avalanche. I watched the black heap up as the notes grew smaller and more crammed together, and as I tried to get ahead, it always overtook me and I stumbled and was lost.

I wanted to play jazz and blues but didn't know how to go about it, so I settled on Fats Waller, and pushed my way through his wry serenades: "Your Feet's Too Big," "I Ain't Got Nobody," "Viper's Drag," "Alligator Crawl," "Honeysuckle Rose." I was given a record of him playing them himself and despaired to hear him be so nimble, all glissando like a speed skater, reaching easily an octave and three, an octave and four, and freeing up the tempo. My versions were English, sturdy and contained, but still, I hoped, had something of his swaggering ugliness. That was what attracted me to this music most.

I bought a book of Scott Joplin's rags because I had seen the film *The Sting*, which featured his rag "The Entertainer." I discovered that I had no interest in playing something I knew so well and found two other pieces in the book—"Bethena," a waltz, and "Solace," a serenade. Joplin insists: "Do not play this piece fast. It is never right to play ragtime fast." I never grew tired of that challenge. Instead of rushing through a passage of Beethoven before being buried under a pile of notes, I had to pull back from the most joyful crescendo I had ever encountered.

It did not seem strange to me to go from the record shop to the music shop, to buy a Buzzcocks single and some Chopin Preludes in the same afternoon. While making my way through Chopin's Prelude in C Minor, I got to the fifth bar and hit a phrase I'd heard before. Not in Chopin, nor among my sheet music, but on a record by Donna Summer—a disco hit I had once owned and now would bury thirty feet down in the woods—"Could It Be Magic?" That phrase is the best part of the Donna Summer song, and the best part of the Prelude too—it starts from somewhere up above and then immediately decays, like the kind of firework that is all about its fall.* But how could this happen? I discovered that the song was written by Barry Manilow, whose ballad "Mandy" I'd briefly been hooked on.

Now Barry and Donna were back to haunt me. I didn't want them, I wanted Chopin (and the Buzzcocks). Yet I couldn't play the Prelude without hearing them (both!) warbling, "Come, come, come into my arms . . ." I was fascinated, too, to think that a songwriter as cheesy as Barry Manilow could be as serious about music as to know Chopin, and cocky enough to steal his phrase. Perhaps Chopin had done such things too. I had thought of Mozart, Beethoven, Chopin as coming fully formed and out of nowhere. Perhaps classical music was like pop and punk after all, in which things were borrowed, stolen, and adapted all the time.

When the family home was sold, that piano was delivered to a housing co-op I was living in near Clapham Junction. We had bare floorboards, mold on the walls, wasteland and corrugated-iron fences around us. In the next ten years, I moved six times

---

*I asked the composer Richard Baker why this phrase was so captivating: "The eight chords in the original (which provide the harmony of Manilow's chorus) are constructed over a chromatically descending bass line, and the inner voices also move by step to create varying degrees of harmonic tension. Resolution is denied until the seventh chord, with the sixth chord in particular calculated to wring maximum harmonic tension: to me, it seems to be hinting at inexpressible yearning, emotions almost too strong to bear."

and took the piano with me. It was always the biggest thing in the room. I lived in tiny flats where I could hear neighbors coughing through the wall, and so I never played it and because I knew I would be out of practice, I wanted to play even less. Finally, I was moving to a top-floor flat where the piano would not fit. It was worn out and got in the way, like an old sick pet.

I found a dealer from Chingford in the Yellow Pages who came by one evening. The piano was in my daughter's room.

"I can't do anything with that," he said.

I was moving out in a week and the piano had to be gone. "Could you just take it away?"

"Not worth it."

In despair, I sat down on the bed, and my daughter copied me.

The dealer was a huge man. He looked on us like a god with a soft spot, put his hand in his pocket, and pulled out the largest wad of notes I've ever seen. "I'll give you fifty quid."

"That's very kind. When do you want to collect it?"

"I'll take it now."

And he did. He shoved the piano into the stairwell, got in front of it, and asked me to push it off the step like a boat from a jetty. He half carried, half dragged it away.

Ten years later, I bought a plain Dutch piano because my daughter had begun to play. I still had my grandmother's piano stool and, in it, my music. My fingers were stiff and slow, but the real problem was that I was thinking about what I was doing. Only when I forgot to concentrate did my body admit that it remembered everything.

# 18

# THE CAT'S WHISKER

*The buzz of earth, buzz of the earth . . .*
—OSIP MANDELSTAM,
"Equipped with the Eyesight and
Absorption of Wasps"

Before I had a record player in my room, I had a transistor radio. My parents issued one to each of us like a form of rations. They were the size of a billy can, with a leather case and loop handle. Before this, I had thought of radio as news and orchestras, background to eating cereal or brushing teeth, to my father reading the paper and my mother sewing. Now I carried around Radio 1 pressed to my ear as if listening to *Top of the Pops* in a seashell. Music became a private occupation, not least because the sound was so small. I could not have shared that radio with anyone even if I'd wanted to.

The radios in the kitchen and living room were ruled by my parents to the extent that it wouldn't have occurred to me to switch one of them on, even when alone. In the car, on those long journeys to Wales, I would grow desperate for music and would plead with my father to let me listen to a pop station. If I got my way, someone would protest, especially because I could not help but sing along. In our holiday cottage, I would survey the bookshelves, seek out a radio, and hunker down. If allowed to, I would not leave the house.

Songs on Radio 1 were happy or silly or romantic, and so were the voices of the daytime DJs; so was life, apparently. I listened to the request shows and thought that everyone who wrote in had their name read out and their record played, and that by listening I was becoming part of a network of happy pop fans who were all attuned to a certain signal.

My brother once made a "cat's whisker," a crystal set with a copper-wire antenna that magically earthed itself and, without batteries or electricity, brought radio so distant and frail that it could only be heard whispering in headphones. The sheer difficulty of this made every utterance precious, and we would listen to anything—Dutch, big band music, Morse code. The reception of my transistor was not much more reliable, and I spent a lot of time tuning it and moving it from desk to floor to window ledge, angling the antenna. And then there would be the miracle of a clear signal, and a song I knew and the possibility of all the other songs that might be played after that. Radio was no longer background noise. I practically sat and watched it.

We had four radio stations, which closed down each night. Then there would be the shipping forecast, the national anthem, and silence. There was plenty of silence although radio was a far leakier medium than television. The airwaves were full of crackle and hiss, and I could pass through all kinds of countries and conversations. Everything was always in midflow—a song, a concert, a rant, an advert, a jingle—as if beyond our early-to-bed shores was a twenty-four-hour world of music and talk.

I could not watch television in the privacy of my room and had to negotiate hard to get to see what I wanted. After bedtime, I couldn't put a light on and read but I could listen to my radio under the blankets. When Abba won the Eurovision Song Contest in 1974, it was all a matter of noise: first the bleariness of live performance then the matted applause, the dramatized announcements, the adding-up of points, the speculation and calculation and the band in interview, breathless, startled, and right there.

As with music itself, I started with the most obvious step, Radio 1, and then looked around for something more interesting and found Radio Luxembourg. It might have been more or less the same as Radio 1 but it had the cachet of being foreign and harder to tune into, which made me feel like a member of a more exclusive club. It also carried advertisements, rare enough then to seem like colorful diversions.

From Radio Luxembourg, I moved on to the pirate station Radio Caroline. It was illegal, and broadcast from a boat just out there off the Essex coast. Listening to Radio Caroline was like eavesdropping on the world of older teenagers. There was no pattern, no sense of organized timed entertainment but something altogether more live. Its DJs never sounded silly or romantic, and rarely cheerful. They were improvisatory and they never played the usual chart hits. They played songs from LPs: Eric Clapton's "Layla," Lynyrd Skynyrd's "Free Bird," Led Zeppelin's "Stairway to Heaven." Instead of adverts, they had spots promoting "Loving Awareness." The DJs talked like people instead of like DJs and when something went wrong, they told you about it. The boat was raided, the generator packed up, or there was a storm and the music would lurch around as if the airwaves were all of a sudden as turbulent as the sea.

The most exciting radio was like this, coming from a distance, out of the dark, and the DJ who always sounded as if he were on the edge of the island, at the top of a tower built out of records, was Radio 1's John Peel. I taped his programs, scribbled notes, and was prepared to listen to anything if he chose to play it. All teenagers who considered themselves serious about music listened to John Peel, only we were far too serious to do what he did for ourselves. We relied on him to take the risks, to stick his neck out, to play something just for the hell of it because it was new and to be tried out, and it didn't matter if by the next week he was bored or proved wrong because there would be more to try, to get excited about, and to give up on, and that was what it was all about.

I stopped listening to music on the radio when I had acquired enough of my own to contrive listening to it as an adventure. Oh, look! This! I haven't heard this for ages! As if my carefully edited stacks of records and tapes might ever spring any kind of real surprise.

# 19

# JOYFUL OCCASIONS

*From the preceding quotations, it will sufficiently appear, 1. That dancing was a religious act, both of the true and also of idol worship. 2. That it was practised exclusively on joyful occasions, such as national festivals or great victories. 3. That it was performed by maidens only. 4. That it was performed usually in the day-time, in the open air in highways, fields, or groves.*
     —DR. LYMAN BEECHAM's tract on dancing
       published by the American Tract Society,
        cited in *May Christians Dance?* by Jas. H. Brookes

Somewhere between twelve and thirteen, I formed a gang of three with Janey and Cara. For the first time, I felt like a girl. It was as if I couldn't have been a girl on my own or with my sister but only if I were connected to other girls. Alone I existed more and more in a perpetual state of embarrassment but with my friends I was a girl, no, we were GIRLS and we went forth into the world arms linked, making noise.

Were we trying to get attention or to scare everyone else

away? We did not smile, we guffawed. We did not sigh, we shrieked. We were never irritated, we were enraged. When we sang, it was as loudly as we could. It was not meant to be serious or beautiful, and while sometimes it might have been to make ourselves feel safe in the dark as we made our way home, we were just as loud in daylight.

If we sang out of trepidation or the need for release, the experience was nonetheless one of joy, as was dancing. I danced in line with my friends and alone in front of the mirror, as a rehearsal of love. It was preparation for saying "Look at me" and "Yes, I will" and "I know how."

There are times when we need the rocket fuel of singing and dancing to power us through an act of blind faith. Falling in love is one of those times, when we need to move into a phase of enchantment with enough force so that when things cool and the air clears, we are locked into that person, that love. We fall in love and we sing as we walk down the street; we turn up the music and dance.

# 20

# THE KITCHEN ARIAS

*My sister had a trenchant way of cutting our bread-and-butter for us, that never varied.*
—CHARLES DICKENS,
**Great Expectations**

We turned nine, eleven, thirteen, and fifteen, and more than anything wanted our own lives. Boredom might drive us together for a game of Monopoly or table tennis but we only really met when slumped in front of the television or around the kitchen table over the evening meal. This was when we talked. Our friends were always welcome and somehow my mother fed everyone. While I was proud of this, I made anxious speeches and issued warnings:

Don't sit there, that's my little brother's chair and only he knows how to . . . Oh! Let me help you up. Sorry, it's just that it's held together by this string here. No, don't worry, you haven't broken it. It fell apart ages ago but he was so attached to it that when Mum got the new ones, she let him keep it. Are you all right? Why don't you sit here. Oh. I'll just

move those plates. They're from yesterday. I didn't wash up,
you see. We won't, or at least Mum says we won't and she's
given up trying so we're each supposed to do our own, only
we forget and so she leaves them on our chairs. She's just
being . . . logical.

During a meal, everyone talked and persisted whether or not
anyone responded, so that it seemed as if each of us were singing
to ourselves:

*There's a fascinating article in the* British Medical Journal *about
    the tapeworm . . .*
*Did you see what Tracey was wearing today?*
*This is ever so nice, Mrs. Greenlaw. What's it called?*
*What is that disgusting notepad doing by the phone?*
*I told you, Mum. I'm, like, a vegetarian.*
*And she's got, you know, child-bearing hips.*
*Now, the tapeworm, as you may know . . .*
*But you, like, shoot things.*
*Boiled wheat and ratatouille.*
*It's advertising thrush. It's disgusting.*
*Do you think I could get away with it?*
*What's thrush?*
*I need a lift into town.*
*I shoot pests.*
*It's just the stationery your father gets sent by pharmaceutical
    companies.*
*It's a yeast infection.*
*They're still animals.*
*Mum, why are there weeds in the salad?*
*I would describe it as the result of an imbalance of vaginal flora.*
*Do you want me waiting alone in the dark for two hours?*
*You can't be vegetarian if you pour gravy all over your potatoes.*

*What about my hips, though?*

*They're dandelions from the lawn.*

*I could be abducted.*

*Don't be silly, we mustn't waste paper.*

*What's vaginal?*

*The French eat them in salad.*

*I'd eat meat if I killed it myself.*

*Mum! What's green and has got six legs and if it falls out of a tree kills you?*

*Should we tell her it doesn't suit her? I mean, it would just be being kind.*

*They call it* pis-en-lit, *which means—*

*Did you kill this ratatouille yourself, then?*

*I've missed the bus now anyway.*

*"Wet the bed." It's actually a diuretic.*

*I don't know, darling. Hasn't it got something to do with a banana?*

# 21

# BROKEN VOICES

*"Where is Bernard?" said Neville. "He has my knife. We were in the tool-shed making boats, and Susan came past the door. And Bernard dropped his boat and went after her taking my knife, the sharp one that cuts the keel. He is like a dangling wire, a broken bell-pull, always twangling."*

—VIRGINIA WOOLF,
*The Waves*

There were 180 pupils in my year at school, girls and boys, thirteen or fourteen, all undergoing monstrous change. Some burst out of their seams while others erupted through their skin. Some slowed down into men and women overnight, and took on gravity. Others found that their circuitry came loose, and while they were slowly being rewired, their hands and mouths did things that shouldn't be seen or said as they blurted, stumbled, and twitched. There were those for whom it was all ooze, blush, sweat, and stink, and those who experienced such silence that even though they could see torment and confusion all around them, they prayed to be afflicted. One or two simply flowered.

Some boys' voices squeaked, some croaked and veered, others descended gently, and it could take weeks or months but then it was done, and they turned to us and spoke.

*So will you*

*Do you want to*

*Y'know*

*If you*

*Will*

*Want*

*Go*

*Out*

*Go out*

*Go out with*

*So?*

# 22

# THE OTHER SIDE OF THE AIR

*when the innermost point in us stands*
*outside, as the most practiced distance, as the other*
*side of the air . . .*

—RAINER MARIA RILKE,
"Music"

We were dancing on a Scottish hillside, a ring of teenagers who had known one another for maybe ten days. This was a dangerous dance, in which someone ended up in the middle and had to choose their next partner. Suddenly I was in the middle and everyone was nudging, giggling, and whispering because there was the boy who had been kissing me and there was the girl he had been involved with a week before and there was the boy she had gone off with and there was the boy who had put his arm around me by the campfire on the first night and there was my friend the sister of the boy whom the girl had gone off with.

For six years, my parents sent us each summer to Forest School Camps where we learned how to build a fire, use a knife, cook porridge, put up a tent in the rain, pack a rucksack, dubbin boots, walk all day in rain, live in mud, shit in a hole in the ground, and play games in the forest at night. We smoked and drank within the limits of our meager allowances and rural isolation. We barely washed and never brushed our hair. We also learned folk songs and country dancing. An alternative outdoors-based school in the 1930s, FSC has persisted with its ethos intact and insisted on such responsibility and freedom that even the most cynical teenager unbent, used the lingo, played the games, sang, and danced.

Hormones hit and all of a sudden I wanted to belong, only not with the serious girls with their kneesocks and violins. I wanted to be desirable and bad, which in Essex at that time meant being a disco girl. I was on the edge of being accepted by this group and arrived at camp the summer I turned fourteen in a state of metamorphosis. My clothes were half hippie, half tart and my accent wavered depending on whom I was talking to. I was also on an intense course of medication for period pain that turned my brain and body to sponge, and I behaved like a sponge—absorbing the spillage of someone else's drama. The boy who put his arm around me was good-looking and nice. The one who kissed me was not, but he was a disco boy. In this world of cheesecloth, denim, and center partings, here was a boy with spiky hair, a bomber jacket, bright tight shirts, and loud-checked baggy trousers. He strutted, swore, smoked, and spat continuously, and I was besotted. One night, we passed in the dark and he said he'd split up with his girl, swore, spat, and kissed me. The next night we met again and kissed some more, and when I asked for a cigarette he grabbed me as if about to throw me and "joked" that he would give me all his cigarettes if I "dropped 'em." I said no and he spat, laughed, and walked off. The next night I let him kiss me again and the day after that he was back with his girl, who sat on a log with her cohorts, queenly and mocking, and taunted me as I queued for my porridge. The boy she'd taken up with meantime, now rejected, came and sat next to me, and for a morning we went through the motions of preferring each other to either of them.

My head ached, my body bloated, and as I became more anxious, more sure that I was being scorned, I grew louder. After two years of being frightened, I had become angry and found that the best way to get people to leave me alone was to scare. At school, I could be tough and remote; I knew where I was. Where was I now? In despair, I stepped away from myself and watched this confused, uncontrollable girl break down and sob and shout, unable to say why because she didn't know. In disgust, I abandoned her. People were kind but exasperated. She was pathetic and annoying, and so childish that even those her own age felt they had permission to offer criticism and advice. "You could be all right, you know, if you . . ." "I'd like you if you didn't . . ." "Why do you wear that?" I wanted to be with them, not her, so stayed away for the duration.

On camp, dancing was the chance for everything whispered to be enacted. It could be as fraught with political implication as an Elizabethan pavane. In two weeks, a court had been established and hostilities declared. There had been hostages, casualties, spies, and traitors, and now there was détente. The camp stood in a ring, hand in hand, and everyone understood and was glad not to be the girl in the middle.

I watched her in that ring. She was aware of the whispering and what it meant, and she knew that the disco boy pouting and winking and miming, "Me, choose me," was doing so in order to amuse his gang. She knew she had been cast in their drama, not even cast—she was less character than prop. In the end, she did what she was being told to do, and chose him, and he laughed and spat and twirled her around, all the time grinning and winking at his girl.

# 23

# THE ELECTRIFIED SELF

*The dancing itself begs description. Every figure lasts about an hour, and the ladies bounce up and down the middle with a degree of spirit which is quite indescribable. As to the gentlemen . . . They whirl their partners round, nothing loath, scrambling up and falling and embracing and knocking up against the other couples until they are fairly tired out and can move no longer. The same scene is repeated again and again, slightly varied, by an occasional row, until a late hour at night. And a great many clerks and apprentices find themselves next morning with aching heads, empty pockets, damaged hats, and a very imperfect recollection of how it was they did not get home.*

—CHARLES DICKENS,
"Country Fair Dance"

I was becoming a girl as instructed by girls but I knew I wasn't a real girl, at least not of this kind. I wanted to be a disco girl like Tina, whose every aspect conformed to some golden section of girldom: her height relative to her shape, her

prettiness relative to her smartness, her niceness relative to her
toughness. Tina offered certainties. She issued instructions on
how to dance, whom to like, and what to wear. Clothes had to be
pressed, shoes polished, bodies scrubbed, shaved, creamed, and
deodorized. Just as her mother kept the house fanatically clean,
so Tina attended to herself. Each morning, her face would be re-
tuned—the brightness turned down, the color turned up—and
she would stride into school, her hips and breasts armoured, her
hair a winged blond helmet. I wanted this shell, which she used
to attract or deflect at will. To me, she was wise and ruthless, a
goddess of war.

What did my family make of the painted, squawking girl I
suddenly became? Nothing. They behaved as if all I'd done was
change the side of my parting or swap the laces in my shoes, certainly nothing worth remarking. I could have come to table wearing a diving suit and doubt anyone would have said more than
"Pass the potatoes." I believed I had found what I wanted to be.
They knew it would pass.

I teetered on platform-wedge shoes, and a pencil skirt cur-
tailed my stride. How these clothes made us walk was how they
made us dance. We minced, jerked, and shuffled; shoulders
hunched, elbows tucked in. We danced in a circle or in line, and
performed routines with the zeal of synchronized swimmers. The
only release we had was in the music, which was just what Tina
would not permit us to be—deadly serious *and* lighthearted.

The disco evening began with a whole other evening's worth
of getting ready. Three or four girls would congregate in someone's bedroom and become hysterical. They milled about in a
vortex of skirts, tops, shoes, tights, mascara, foundation, eyeliner,
nail polish . . . The air was weighed down by our perfumes, which
claimed to smell of melon or apple or peach. They were as un-
ripe as we were. We would share out face packs, which set in a

yellow or green gelatinous mask. I peeled mine off too roughly and it left my skin bright pink, my spots inflamed. Legs and armpits were inspected for any hair that had missed the razor, eyebrows scrutinized. Makeup was all about the eyes, three shades plus liner, three coats of mascara. Hair was blown dry and tonged into flicks then lacquered to toughness with extra-hold hairspray that smelled like a bag of cheap sweets. We were drawn together in the whirl of preparation and remained so. We strode down the street three abreast, squeezed onto the bus seat, walked into the hall arms linked. We danced, raised our glasses, and lit our cigarettes together; we shrieked, pointed, whispered, and giggled as one.

These discos took place in village halls—raised, wooden, low-roofed constructions designed for council meetings and jumble sales. They were strip-lit rooms whose windows were jammed shut, and they smelled of cedar floor polish, wet wool, disinfectant, and gravy. There would be a stage, where the DJ set up, and a kitchen from where soft drinks would be sold in paper cups. We bought the orange squash and topped it up with vodka from our handbags, or emptied the cup and filled it with cider. Drinking wasn't as imperative at a disco as it was at a party. There was too much to do.

Safely in place in our circles and lines, under cover of maximum volume, within the bounds of our pencil skirts, we could be fierce. Imagine ten girls in four-inch wedge heels stomping in time to War's "Me and Baby Brother"—hop, skip, jump, CRASH . . . For me, disco was a new chemistry, geometry, architecture, and physics. The village and its landscape were locked in place, and I within them, until the bass beat opened up the earth, the brass section blew off the roof, and you had to move, everything had to start moving and, to quote Brass Construction, "Keep on Movin'."

The DJs were not personalities. They were doing a job and gave us what we expected and asked for. They set up their decks, lined up their boxes of records, said little, and produced the same sequence every time.

1. The familiar, friendly introduction—Abba's "Dancing Queen."
2. The full-on funk once the girls had overcome their nerves—K.C. and the Sunshine Band, Disco Tex and the Sex-O-Lettes, Earth Wind & Fire.
3. Ska to persuade some of the boys to join them—"Johnny Reggae," "Al Capone."
4. A break for novelty records so the boys who couldn't dance could take over the floor and lurch about—"The Laughing Gnome," "The Wurzel Song."
5. Advanced—David Bowie's "Heroes" or "Golden Years," so that the serious dancers didn't get bored.
6. Light new dance with a restricted beat that the boys could jig about to, bringing them into contact— Van McCoy and the Soul City Symphony's "The Hustle."
7. Preparation for the slow dance—The Floaters' "Float On."
8. Something that could be a slow dance, or not—The Commodores' "Sunday Morning."
9. The actual slow dance—Chicago's "If You Leave Me Now."
10. Could be a slow dance or something for the loners in the corner—The Moody Blues' "Nights in White Satin."
11. Recovery—Marvin Gaye's "Got to Give It Up."
12. Sing along and go home smiling—Jeff Beck's "Hi-Ho Silver Lining."

If I had not kissed anyone, or danced with anyone, or had a reason to cry, the music made me feel as if I had gone through all that anyway. Because the music was charged and we were no more singular than iron filings, no less easily moved as the music attracted and repelled, organized and disturbed and then let us into the night, clusters of emotion ready to dissolve into sleep.

# 24

# THE SLOW DANCE

*Only on horseback and in the mazurka was Denisov's short stature not noticeable and he looked the dashing fellow he felt himself to be.*

—LEO TOLSTOY,
*War and Peace*

As a student, whenever I came home I would read the births, marriages, and deaths columns of the local paper. There was always a whole page of weddings, with photographs. The brides were often taller and bigger than the grooms, but maybe that was because they were in frothy white with their hair up, festooned with flowers and lace, whereas the men wore morning suits of newsprint gray, and still favored lank shoulder-length cuts. They always struck the same pose and had the same expression, as if copying the figures on top of their cake. "Turn toward each other," the photographer would have commanded, "but look at the camera. And smile! It's your wedding day, remember? Hold hands, no, not like that . . ." They might be seventeen or eighteen and were learning how a husband and wife should stand.

I always found people I knew, not just in those columns but among the small ads as well. Names caught my eye because they were those of the slow dancers. Barry Wise now advertised reproduction antiques, Martin Love announced that he was taking over his father's scrap-metal yard, and little Danny English had passed his catering qualifications and was rejigging the menu at the Lion and Lamb. Andy Bellman had been arrested for being drunk and disorderly, Kevin Birleigh was caught shoplifting women's underwear, and Terry Elm had been killed while playing an old game—driving at night with no lights across a junction. I would find the names of the slow dancers in the cemeteries, too—illness and accident and those who had done what they could to break out of a quiet life.

At fourteen I had even less in common with these boys than with the disco gang I was working so hard to be part of. We didn't have anything to say and when we passed in the street or at school, they smirked and I blushed. But I fell in love at the village-hall discos because they could dance. Unlike the clever, excruciated boys who were my friends, they knew how to be boys.

Although girls talked about boys, we danced for ourselves and one another. Boys loomed out of the shadows during the opening bars of the first slow dance, which might be the Chi-Lites' "Have You Seen Her?" with its repeated ponderous intro acting as subtitles to what passed between us and the boys who were crossing the floor: "Aaaaaah! . . . Hhhh-mmmm . . ." We simpered and wilted—there would be no stamping or clapping now.

The girls tried to look both occupied and available—whispering but opening out from their knots and circles. As a boy crossed the floor, he grew either taller or smaller. He was either desirable or not. It had nothing to do with personality and not much to do with the detail of his looks.

If the wrong boy's hands were parked on the wrong girl's

lower back, he would stand rigidly apart and commence to maneuver her around in a circle regardless of tempo. Or he would push his luck, grab her bottom and pull her in, and she would jerk away and dance with her hands on his shoulders, keeping him back. They gazed at the floor between their feet or over one another's shoulders at their friends but did not give up—at least they were dancing.

The right boy with the right girl would not have to think about how to approach the dance. It just happened, you just were, and all the thoughts you'd had about this moment, how you intended to be or intended him to be, were gone. You didn't think at all because this wasn't dancing but being moved, and you felt the heat and pressure of his body against you and the heat and pressure inside you, another kind of electrification that was not about music at all.

# 25

# AS IF IN SPACE

*Ourselves in the tune as if in space . . .*
—WALLACE STEVENS,
"The Man with the Blue Guitar"

The boys we really wanted to dance with were not those who sat next to us at school but the older ones, who had jobs and behaved like men. Most left school at fifteen to follow their fathers onto farms and into factories, or to take their place in the family firm of roofers, scrap-metal dealers, or greengrocers. They were almost the last apprentices, training as printers, butchers, and carpenters. Like Wheelwright, Burgess, and Cooper, these trades were also local surnames; thirty years on, they seem almost as quaint.

These boys learned to drive when they were about twelve, in someone's field or along the one stretch of straight road out by the reservoir. At seventeen, they could do so legally, and now that they had jobs, they could afford cars. They would swagger into the pub swinging their key fobs and then slamming them down on the table, like gauntlets. Outside, the lane was full of Heralds and Cortinas—cars with chivalric names, which the boy racers had patched together and souped up. They fitted them with new cassette decks and stereo speakers. After all, what was the point of going fast if you couldn't make noise?

The summer I first knew boys with cars was astounding. To leave the village just like that, without having to wait two hours for a bus, and then travel so fast. Word would go around the pub that there was a party ten miles away and we would cram into someone's car, two on the passenger seat and three boys in the back with girls on their knees, and we would be there just like that.

The boy drove fast. He wanted the girls to bounce and scream, and we did. If the other boys said anything at all it was to urge him to drive faster, or to turn off his lights as he crossed a junction, or to take a corner on the wrong side of the road. Two boys died this way, coming around a blind corner into the path of a double-decker bus. We were shocked, but not touched: it seemed no more likely that such a thing could happen to us.

This swerving through the dark felt like liftoff. The car was a bubble of noise and light that collapsed all the distances and flew through the dark fields that had kept me so marooned. Some nights the driving around became the whole point and we would flit and zip from pub to pub, party to party, wanting to keep moving just because we could.

Essex, though flat, is not straightforward. To the north, the land has readily submitted to Roman roads, highways, and single fields as broad as the view. Essex is resistant. You see your destination long before you reach it. The back lanes through those fields are all hairpin bends and humpback bridges. Hedgerows tower and trees throw out awkward branches. Roads twist around copses, paths are eroded or overgrown, and fields either brim with crops or erupt under the plow. I felt so perpetually thwarted that if I came across open ground I would run for the sake of it. I never got anywhere even then.

In the car, we needed music in order to feel how fast we were going, and for these boys, that meant heavy metal: Led Zeppelin, Deep Purple, Black Sabbath—all juggernaut bass lines and skidding lead-guitar breaks, the volume turned up so high that a song would lose shape and I would feel rather than hear it. Everything shook—the car, my body, and the world outside, as if by sheer force of sound we could make every empty church, closed shop, locked gate, and lurking police car rattle and vibrate until they came apart and the world was nothing but parts, all up in the air.

Too young to bring about change, we brought about disturbance. Heavy metal was our engine noise—it was trucks on the cricket field, bulldozers tearing up the green, boots stomping on flower beds, cars driven through hedges, the only thing that could tear a hole in the silence of a Sunday afternoon.

Sometimes the boy driving turned on the radio and we girls would sing along to some anthem from our disco nights that was crackly and distorted as if it had rushed too fast across space: "I can't li-i-i-i-ve . . . if living is without yo-ooo-ou . . ." Now it was not so much a song as a continuum, a booming tunnel of desire through which we flew like static.

In the dark, music was our landscape as much as our map. The real daylight map was less interesting than its contortions might suggest. There are no proper hills in Essex and so we were like the Dutch who used to have to climb a church tower in order to see the view. We lived in a world that was two-thirds sky. How to get up in the air? One night Robbie drove us to the top of a multistory car park. He turned up Black Sabbath and then raced down the narrow switchback of the exit ramp. He threw the car around each corner as if the ramp were nothing but cor-

ners, and we swerved and swerved, almost bouncing off the concrete walls. Was I scared? No. I remember it as a moment of pure
pleasure driven and held by the blast of that music which had
propelled us like a rocket through the exosphere until we broke
through gravity and were nothing more than sound in space.

# 26

# SPIRITS

*The Greek name for a butterfly is Psyche, and the same word means the soul. There is no illustration of the immortality of the soul so striking and beautiful as the butterfly, bursting on brilliant wings from the tomb in which it has lain, after a dull, grovelling, caterpillar existence, to flutter in the blaze of day and feed on the most fragrant and delicate productions of the spring. Psyche, then, is the human soul, which is purified by sufferings and misfortunes, and is thus prepared for the enjoyment of true and pure happiness.*

—THOMAS BULFINCH,
*Mythology: The Age of Fable*

**D**rinking was another way to swerve through the dark, although the initial reason I drank was to still myself. Here was the larger world I had dreamed of, but just as I had rushed through childhood, the world seemed now to rush through me and kept me in a flutter. I felt too insubstantial to hold my place. The bright, loud room had opened its door, but to make my way through that loaded air felt like pushing through waves.

Cara's father had a cupboardful of lurid, dusty bottles brought back from holidays abroad. Boyish and medicated, he had had two heart attacks before the age of forty and was given to outbursts of fury and subsequent outbursts of love. He did not often drink and routinely accused his children of stealing his alcohol behind his back. (Janey's mother made notches in the labels of her sherry and vodka bottles, which Janey topped up with water, whereas when my mother noticed the whiskey disappearing, she said something so gentle that I never took anything again.)

"He wouldn't notice if we just took a little of each." Cara found an empty medicine bottle, which Janey and I helped her fill with all the colors and flavors that the cupboard contained. It settled into a bitter brown syrup much like cough linctus.

We set off for the youth-club disco but decided to drink the bottle at the recreation ground first. We wanted, needed, to be drunk before we arrived. It must have been spring because I remember being struck by the softness of the evening. We sat on the swings feeling ironic and grown-up, and passing the sticky bottle back and forth, and we sang hard, comical versions of the songs of the slow dances—"If You Leave Me Now" and "Have You Seen Her?"—laughing at the very idea of them. I felt grown-up enough to act the child and swung higher than anyone. The darkness rose and fell around me and then concentrated itself into a series of slamming doors as my vision blackened. I hadn't even noticed myself getting drunk and now I could hardly see.

The youth club was shockingly well lit but the music was loud and I loved the music and there were my friends, Tina and Julie and Dawn, and I loved them. The room fell away but the music stayed in place and I loved the music so I danced and all the while kept laughing because I had not stopped swinging and

falling and was farther outside myself than I had ever been and
Julie who I wanted so much to be my friend was dancing with me
and we stepped toward each other and back and clapped and
turned and stepped together again and she was laughing too
and I threw my head back and then fell forward into Julie's smile
and when I looked up people frowned and turned away and
someone was shouting and my face was wet and I couldn't see.

I was led to a bathroom where the woman who ran the youth
club held a cloth against my face, which was covered in blood.
Julie's teeth had sliced across my nose. There were voices behind
me: "Is it broken? Has she broken her nose?" When I heard that,
I looked into the mirror and tried to focus through my drunk-
enness and shock, sure I would see a monster. My nose was
unchanged and the face I saw was mine but this was not a
reflection. It was too far away, more like some inner self that had
slipped free and looked back at me now with my own fundamental sadness.

My mother was called and came to take me home. She reacted as she always did to such emergencies, with detached prac-
ticality, and I was so grateful that she was neither furious nor
distressed that I didn't realize till later how much I wanted someone to reassure or punish me. Nor did I think about the possibility that she was simply controlling her feelings. I didn't yet know
that that was something we can do. Nothing was said. If ever anything was said in such situations, it was said once and quietly, and
it had more impact than any amount of yelling would have done.

The bleeding stopped and she explained that I had not broken my nose and would not need stitches. She taped the cut together with what she called a "butterfly dressing" and I stared
into the mirror again, amazed that those two thin strips of plaster could hold me together.

# 27

# ANOTHER TEN SECONDS

*"I really neither hate nor like it," Ethel told Lou.
"It just doesn't seem nearly as jolly as the tunes we
had when I was a girl."*

*"Mother says we have all the same tunes, but
not played so well," Lou said.*

—ELIZABETH TAYLOR,
*In a Summer Season*

When punk came to town it didn't take any notice of me and I failed to go out and meet it, but it left behind a sense of disturbance that affected only certain people. It was as if it hit their natural resonant frequency and set something off, the way a car starts to shake when it reaches a particular speed.

By the summer of 1976 we had heard of punk rock, only we hadn't really heard it. We lived just thirty-five miles outside London, but at that time such news traveled slowly. And then, in September, punk turned up and bounced around our town like a stage fight around a set. Eddie and the Hot Rods, who turned out to be more or less local, played in Chelmsford's football stadium along with Chelsea and the Damned, only six miles from our school. There was some kind of standoff, and I think the Damned went home without performing. I didn't know anyone who went but there was said to have been a riot, and I remember the excitement at school that this thing was out there, close by, possibly dangerous, and above all that it was something that might be for us.

Three months later, I was watching television after school and there was Bill Grundy, presenter of *Thames Today*, sweatily baiting the Sex Pistols. He behaved like a teacher who had taken the sixth form to the pub and was now punishing them for not being his friends:

> *Grundy:* Go on, you've got another ten seconds. Say something outrageous.
> *Steve:* You dirty bastard.
> *Grundy:* Go on, again.
> *Steve:* You dirty fucker!
> *Grundy:* What a clever boy.
> *Steve:* You fucking rotter!
> *Grundy (to the camera):* Well, that's it for tonight. I'll be seeing you soon. I hope I'll not be seeing you [the band] again. From me, though, goodnight.

Punk did not emerge into an unformed musical world and those making their way toward it were given time to get there. Crowds were a mix of the shaven, spiked, pierced hardcore and those who had just gotten around to ripping a few holes in their school blazers. The hippies and soul boys, the glam rockers were all still much in evidence, and television captured this too. Look at the audiences. It would take me more than another year to look like anything approaching a punk, and I never looked more than punkish. The first thing I did was buy a pair of straight-legged jeans, which were so new to Essex that when I wore them to the youth club, I was mocked. I did not have the nerve to do this alone, but had gone into the shop with Janey and Cara and we all three bought them, more or less as a dare. Even so, I was surprised to find that when people laughed at me, I didn't care. After three years of trying to fit in, I liked the idea of being different.

The music I was beginning to listen to gave me a new sense of shape—straight lines, clean lines. I had tried hard to be a girl but it was tiring and often went wrong. In the ten seconds it took to decide to go into that shop, I had made up my mind. Why try anymore?

One night Cara came back with me after a party. We were laughing at the people who'd been there—the giggling girls and posing boys, the terrible music and lack of drink. We didn't want to be part of all that anymore, but for now there was nowhere else to go. The least we could do was try harder to look different. "I'm sick of my hair," Cara said. It had been cut into a sophisticated bob, which made girls whisper admiringly, and boys who had not noticed her before whistle and stare. It brought out the strong foreign beauty of her face, and it was very grown-up. "Cut it off," she said. I had a job in a hairdresser's on Saturdays and while all I did was shampoo the customers, people thought I now knew something about cutting hair. I didn't deny it. It was the same being a doctor's daughter: friends showed me their rashes and told me their symptoms, and I came up with a diagnosis. I went to find the surgical scissors we used for cutting paper (just as we used surgical gloves when washing up, and old pharmacy bottles for storing oil and vinegar).

Cara opened a bottle of wine that we'd stolen from the party and put a stack of singles on the gramophone. I started to cut, trying to remember the angle at which I'd seen Louise hold her scissors when making layers, how she held a section of hair up with a comb and snipped jerkily at the tips. I cropped Cara's hair into wisps and spikes, and somehow it worked or at least Cara was beautiful enough to carry it off. We cut my hair between us and stood side by side looking at our open faces. We were eyes and mouths and bones—as simple as that.

The singles plonked onto the turntable, one after the other, but we took no notice. They were songs we didn't want to hear anymore. Squealing dance numbers such as "Shame, Shame, Shame" and theatrical growls, Wild Cherry's "Play That Funky Music," they seemed as old-fashioned and ornate as Victorian mahogany or rococo gilt. It was glass we wanted, clarity and sharpness. We wanted austerity, and we wanted to be taken seriously.

A couple of months later, Cara's hair had grown out so we decided to do it again. I was drunk, careless, overconfident, and all of a sudden she had an odd-looking bald patch on one side. I hastily cropped the hair around it, hoping to blend it in. Cara let me keep trying and this time she didn't look gamine and punky, but mad. She wasn't angry. We convinced each other that the bald patches weren't all that noticeable and anyway it would grow out soon.

At school, girls cackled behind their hands while boys roared. Cara did not react. She didn't seem upset and she was still not angry. I was horrified. If I had slowed down, taken more care, or even stopped, but I had gone on cutting, getting more careless.

The next day, Cara didn't show up. At six o'clock that evening the telephone rang and I answered it, but no one spoke. This happened twice more before I heard the voice of Francesca, Cara's older sister. She was sorry to have put the phone down before but she hadn't known what to say. Cara was in the hospital. When her father had seen her hair, he had said he would not be seen with her in the street, and that he was ashamed and disgusted. She was never to see me again. And so Cara, who would take lifts from strangers and walk through woods alone in the dark, went upstairs and swallowed all her father's pills. She had been found unconscious beside a bus stop.

"She is in a coma," Francesca said. "She has a fifty-fifty chance of waking up and a seventy-five percent chance of brain damage." I tried to make sense of these numbers as "Maybe," "Probably," or "Perhaps" but they all became "What if? What if?" How long had she taken to decide to do it? I was told to wait, that there was nothing to do but wait. I walked into the kitchen and told my parents, and they became grave and distant. Perhaps they were responding as doctors, switching into emergency mode. Or they were conditioned by the dramas of this child to respond to her this way. I turned around and walked out without expecting more and wandered through the house, hoping that while the doctors might be taking hold of the situation, someone might take hold of me. I went upstairs and sat on my bed and cried. My sister came in, burst into tears, turned around, and went out again. I went downstairs and turned on the television, and there was someone singing, then someone talking, and then someone singing, and I couldn't understand why they didn't all stop and gasp and cry.

# 28

# THE WHITE ROOM (I)

*Then Home let us hasten, while yet we can see,*
*For no Watchman is waiting for you and for me.*
—WILLIAM ROSCOE,
"The Butterfly's Ball, and the Grasshopper's Feast"

We liked to swerve through darkness but we had been carried by light and noise, and we had done it together. Now Cara had gone beyond me, and while she recovered, I never caught up with her again. We spoke of it once, several months later.

"Why did you do it?"

"To see what it was like."

After three days, Cara woke up and I was allowed to see her. The signs for Intensive Care led me along a corridor and along a corridor and along . . . It seemed that her room was not in the hospital at all but somewhere out in space.

She looked like herself and in my nervousness I behaved as if this room with a bed in it were just another bedroom, a place where we would giggle and conspire. I told her jokes, passed on gossip, and recounted something funny from the problem page of a magazine. As she lay there trying to smile, I went on trying to be us.

She wasn't us anymore. Her eyes were open and she whispered the odd remark, but she was still off in the dark and somehow reluctant to come back. I stopped talking. How often did we sit in silence? Nurses came and went, and I sat there feeling like a child.

The machines lined up beside Cara's bed understood her better than I did now. They knew what she wanted and how to behave. I let her go back to sleep, and sat and watched the rise and fall on a screen, hoping it to be the folding and opening of her guarded breath.

If only I could have turned a switch on one of the machines and had the white room fill with music. Only what music could relieve this? Cara had taken herself off into the deepest possible silence. We knew now that when you tried to move faster and feel more, it could happen just like that. No wonder we turned the music right up.

# 29

# AN EXUBERANCE

*It may be possible to do without dancing entirely.
Instances have been known of young people passing
many, many months successively without being at
any ball of any description, and no material injury
accrue either to body or mind . . .*

—JANE AUSTEN,
*Emma*

I t was still early 1977 and I was still fourteen but I had
stopped singing in the streets. I didn't cry in the lavatories or
drink till I was sick, and I was no longer interested in love
bites or dance routines. The girls with whom I had shared mirrors, loitered at bus stops, and danced in line were strangers.
Our separation was subtle, mutual, and absolute; one day we met
and simply did not recognize one another.

Tina passed me in the school corridor one afternoon. She
came toward me looking like herself but as she went by, I saw her
differently. The tough bright shell she used to attract or deflect
now seemed constricting. She carried herself like someone with
nothing to hide, but her expression was becoming that of her

mother, a hurt sneer that said many things but above all, "What are you looking at? There's nothing wrong with *me.*" I had hoped to learn from Tina how to be a girl, how to grow up, how to bring my life to life, but now there seemed nothing lively about her.

Her feet wobbled on platform-wedge shoes and her pencil skirt reduced her strut to the trot of an overwound toy. Had our dancing been so full of anger? It now strikes me as despair. The clever ones like Tina were among the brightest girls in the year but they were careful not to show it. None of them talked about going to university or even about leaving home, and no one suggested such things to them either.

If Tina had taken any notice of me, she would have seen a skinny girl in big boots and a torn army jacket covered in scribbled quotations. My hair was a mess, my face undefined. Tina would have thought me scruffy and pretentious, and she'd have been right. I knew that I had let her down, not by defecting so much as by never having measured up in the first place. My father recently told me that he had come across a photo of me at fourteen and had thought to send it to my daughter but something in my face made him decide not to. I know what it was—the desperation and failure showed. It was as if some kid had been given a Teenage Girl kit with a picture of Tina on the box, and I was the botched result.

What happened? There was no revelation, no decision. I had stopped dancing, and would not do so again on a disco floor with a group of girls, all trying to look and move alike. There would be no more giggling and shrieking, and things would cease to be mostly either mortifying or hilarious. It was as if some electrified self had been unplugged along with the disco lights.

I was glad of the rest but another kind of dimming occurred at the same time. When I came back to school that autumn for my O-level year, I would find that I had stopped being able to learn. Part of this was willful—I played truant and refused to work—but something else had happened, a seizing up or slowing down that coincided with the end of dancing.

Recent neuroscience has shown that in puberty there is a surge of gray matter called an "exuberance," an overload of capacity and possibility that enables us to grasp trigonometry in an afternoon or read a Russian novel in a day. It also makes us want to steal a car or save the world or, in my case, drink, cry, scream, sing, and dance. And then there is another surge, but this time of myelin, which insulates the brain's electrical signals, ensuring they stick to the right path and increasing their speed. So we think, and act, less wildly but more clearly.

When Cara came back to school, she too was no longer part of the disco gang. Her overdose would have been too much for Tina, too unseemly. Cara's boyfriend, who was Tina's cousin, was worried and attentive but could not reach her and drifted away. We were at the end of our exuberance.

While I have no memory of throwing out my high heels and hairspray, I do remember the thoroughness with which I was soon to set about getting rid of my disco and soul records. There were a few I couldn't bear to throw out so I hid them at the back of a cupboard, with real fear of their being found. I had an extreme but abstract fear of exposure—just like Tina. In my case, it was not about what I looked like but what I listened to. If someone found Marvin Gaye or the Chi-Lites in my room they would discover something *terrible* about me. But what? And what was I going to listen to now?

# 30

# THE WHITE ROOM (2)

*Let the unmelting snow*
*Lie on black fields forever . . .*
—OSIP MANDELSTAM,
"The Staff"

I t was a small flat above a shop but the living room—entirely white with a deep white carpet—seemed vast. I remember no details, no chairs or pictures or windows, just this whiteness and softness, and a stereo of such power and clarity that I felt as if the music I listened to at home must be a shriveled version of itself. Here, that music was lushly rehydrated. We four, two boys and two girls, each sat against a separate wall, relaxed and apart, not drinking but sharing a joint, and I realized that I was in a room with boys and music but nothing was meant to happen.*

Nick played soul—songs I listened to while dancing, flirting,

---

*Years later, I saw Jim Cartwright's play *Road*, in which two men ask two women back to a flat where they hand out bottles of wine and put on Otis Redding's "Try a Little Tenderness." The women, the audience, wait for the inevitable moves to be made but nothing happens. The four sit, as we did, apart and in silence.

crying, studying, or putting on makeup. Even when I was doing nothing I was still not really listening, still thinking about something else. As a rule of thumb, rock was for boys and disco was for girls, but soul was a place we might meet. America was still far away and English soul was like English jazz or disco, unconvincing. Soul was Marvin Gaye, Otis Redding, Aretha Franklin, Eddie Floyd, Teddy Pendergrass, Wilson Pickett, Percy Sledge. In England, these would be the names of priests, gardeners, farmers, teachers, and grandparents, but coming from America wiped them of association. What these people looked like, how old they were, their names, meant nothing. Soul was about voice and authenticity, and to us these were real singers and this real music, a serious pleasure.

I was already serious about music, by which I mean I did not have to think about whether or not to listen to it. It was part of the day's machine. Despite this, at fourteen I had rarely concentrated as I did that night in the white room over the shop, for once not using music in order to feel things. The song I remember from that evening is not in the end Otis Redding or Wilson Pickett, not even real soul, but Earth Wind & Fire's "That's the Way of the World," a ballad so shrewdly orchestrated that it can balance one teetering hyperbole on top of another. I am still not tired of listening to it and think this has to do with its expanse. In that room it went on forever, not in terms of time but of space. It filled the white room with space so that I was farther and farther away from everyone else and deeper into the blank realm of pure happiness. As soon as the music ended and someone spoke, I would have to step back outside.

# 31

# TOWARDS MUSIC

*The conversation drifted, as it always did, towards
music.*

—JONATHAN COE,
*The Rotters' Club*

We walked into the English countryside winter's night
because someone had told someone who'd told one
of us that in a house at the end of a lane or past a
farm or beyond a wood was a party. No one would give us a lift
and none of us could drive, so we set out as the crow flies across
the fields. In absolute darkness we stumbled over plowed and
frozen earth, slipping from ridge to rut, laughing and falling
and calling to one another because we could not see beyond
ourselves.

Released from the etiquette of disco, I had relaxed. I stopped
giggling, stopped crying, and started to pay attention to boys I
didn't find attractive but interesting. As for music, I sat down and
started listening. The interesting boys did not sing along, they
discussed; or they said nothing but would smile and nod because

they *knew*. They weren't dancers or footballers and could neither flirt nor drive. None of these boys had cars but they had stereos, record collections, amplifiers, and instruments. Their tastes were a mixture of hippie, heavy metal, and esoteric, which included a little punk. They dressed quietly, even negligently; what mattered to them was talk. They had never been any good at football or fighting and so communicated through arias from Monty Python and Derek and Clive. Someone only had to mutter an opening phrase and a dozen boys would launch into the Dead Parrot sketch or "The Lumberjack Song." In that dingy school, that dull town, during those endless afternoons, they got laughs every time. They would discover that being clever and funny worked with girls, only it couldn't yet because they were still bludgeoned by their own chemistry.

We gave up dancing, the boys stopped repeating themselves, and everyone calmed down. In those last years of school, we formed an acerbic but tolerant gang. The parties we went to were smaller and the music quieter. People sat around and talked, smoked, and listened to Bob Dylan or "Stairway to Heaven."

We talked about Devo, Blondie, and the Damned. Punk had taken hold in London and Liverpool. Soon we would start buying the records and going to see the bands but first there was a lull, as if we had to get used to the idea.

Luke had been a fat boy but always cool. He never tried too hard, and was funnier than anyone else. On sunny afternoons, his end of his parents' bungalow was a fug of smoke and pounding rock. I don't think he ever drew his curtains—at least I don't remember a window. His mother would bring us trays of tea and cake as if Luke were entertaining in a front parlor instead of slumped on his bedroom floor rolling joints on the cover of Led Zeppelin's *Physical Graffiti*.

Over the next few years Luke and I spent hours in that room.
We talked about love and death and the world and other people,
but always while listening to music. We were so companionable
that each would forget the other was there and behave as if listening alone: I'd sway and sing along while Luke, a drummer,
tapped and slapped out rhythms as another boy might play air
guitar. (Why did girls never play air guitar? Did we sing along because singing was what girls did or was it that girls only sang because they didn't play air guitar? These are not questions I asked
myself at the time. I was pushing away such complications.)

Luke was passionate about what he liked, scornful of what he
didn't, and open to everything except jazz and soul. I had
thought of music as being the same as style: you were a type and
you stuck to it. You couldn't be devoted to heavy metal but also
enjoy punk, only Luke did and so we would follow Led Zeppelin
with Blondie, and I would relax and admit that I actually liked
Joe Cocker's "With a Little Help from My Friends" live at Woodstock and could we put it on—only it really started to drag and
here was the Cars' "My Best Friend's Girl" . . . Luke showed me
that loving music didn't have to mean wanting the same song all
the time, or believing it perfect, and that what you loved didn't
have to add up, let alone define you.

Why leave this in order to go to a party? It would be like all
parties: a boy lying on the grass next to a pool of vomit, a girl crying on the stairs. The house would be bleary and smoky and too
dark because all the candles had burned down hours ago. Couples would have installed themselves on cushions and sofas, and
would writhe ritually in the shadows. There might be boys and
girls sitting together talking and listening to music, and while
Luke and I were like them, we refused any affinity. We would go
straight to the kitchen and requisition whatever bottles or cans
we found. We set up in a corner near the stereo and, where we
could, took over the music. We liked to sneer at the party and

rarely stayed long. When we decided to go we would return to the kitchen, grab another bottle each, and begin the walk home.

Why did we search out these parties when all we would do was continue the conversations of his room? Perhaps we had to take our idea of ourselves out into the world, or prove our independence. Had it been worth it? Somehow it had.

# 32

# TWELVE COPIES OF THE SAME ORIGINAL

*All the candour of youth was there, as well as all youth's passionate purity. One felt that he had kept himself unspotted from the world.*

—OSCAR WILDE,
*The Picture of Dorian Gray*

I took for granted that I had a room of my own and that I could do with it what I wanted. It had a sloping ceiling and two windows at floor level overlooking the village green. People made jokes about being able to see in as they went past on the bus so I went up into the attic, found some darker, heavier curtains, and kept them shut.

Most of the time I was at home I spent in my room—listening to music, reading, and either avoiding or interrogating myself. The room filled up with my father's Russian novels and American poetry, with disco clothes and then jumble-sale clothes, moldering coffee cups and newspapers. I had a full-length mirror that stood in for the rest of the world. I would dance and sing in front of it, but rarely considered my reflection. I ignored my body as much as I could and concentrated on surfaces. All my attention went into clothes, hair, and makeup.

The walls of my room became the place where I asserted myself. In the first year in Essex, when I was eleven, I painted grotesque versions of cartoon animals behind my bed. Cold, I bashed through the plasterboard covering the fireplace to discover there was no longer a hearth. I put up posters of the Bay City Rollers, as did my sister. When we fought, she cut off my favorite Roller's head. The putting-up and ripping-down of pop stars began to happen more and more frequently as I accelerated through adolescence.

When we were thirteen, Janey had briefly turned me and Cara into fans of Elton John because her father worked for his record label (which I found astounding even though I didn't really know what a record label was) and so she had all his albums. We didn't know how to go out and find pop stars and here one was. Her room was covered in pictures of him, and then one day in a collective shift and without discussion we found that we all three had moved on.

"Elton's crap."

"Yeah."

"So why's he all over your room?"

"Dunno."

"Let's take him down."

"Yeah."

And we did, pulling and tearing and shredding until we couldn't see him anymore. Her bare walls were shocking. What would she put up next? I don't know, because taking down those posters was the last thing I remember doing in Janey's room. It was as if tracks had been switched and we would meet less, talk less, move apart.

The official pinups of teen magazines were as consistent as

eighteenth-century portraiture.* David Essex, David Cassidy, even David Bowie looked pretty much alike from the other side of my room. Their enlarged, immobilized faces were like tepid wax or drying plaster. They had a suggestion of life and warmth but the more you looked, the less they looked back. They peered wistfully past you or, if gazing directly into the lens, would lower their heads and look up with a doggish gaze. Bands stood around like eighteenth-century families, conscious of their position in the group and not sure what to do with their hands. In some shots they were lined up like football teams, and duly folded their arms and demonstrated inexhaustible grins. They were usually placed in front of a vague pastel background or outdoors among, and sometimes in, trees. We were rarely given them as we wanted to see them—playing music.

After the pinups, I became more interested in gravitas. I put up a copy of "Desiderata" ("Go placidly amid the noise and haste . . .") not because I liked what it said but because I liked the smoky late-night design, purple and black with louche flared type. I tried out a poster of one of the album covers drawn by Roger Dean for Yes. I never listened to Yes, but people talked about Roger Dean. My poster was a cartoon of the edge of the world, and returned me to my childhood curiosity about finding myself in such a place.

Punk did not lend itself to pinups. If a band posed for a picture, they stuck their tongues out and put their fingers up. The *New Musical Express* was my source of imagery by then, and it was monochrome newsprint. I started cutting things out and gluing them onto a wall, making a collage. Bands were disarranged, the unknown and the famous indistinguishable. I had no names for most of those I included. The wall was a random collection of im-

---

*"At a distance one would take a dozen of their portraits for twelve copies of the same original . . . they all have the same neck, the same arms, the same coloring, and the same attitude." —J. B. le Blanc, *Letters on the English and French Nations*, 1747.

ages thrown together and allowed to expand until it filled up the available space, somewhat like the music.

The last poster I put up, just a few months before I left home, came with the second Pop Group album, *For How Much Longer Do We Tolerate Mass Murder?* It featured images of famine, torture, and murder alongside such statements as "Nixon and Kissinger should be tried for war crimes" and "Just heard that President Carter is threatening military intervention. American aircraft carriers are heading for Iran." There were details of British police brutality on one side and Abba and the Beatles on the other, captioned "Escapism is not freedom." If I had liked the record more, I might have taken more notice of what the poster said.

# 33

# SILVER JUBILEE

*Here, where the Sommer is so little seene . . .*
—SIR WILLIAM DAVENANT,
"To the Queene, entertain'd at night
by the Countesse of Anglesey"

In June 1977, the Queen celebrated twenty-five years on the throne and I was arguing with my mother about the Union Jack. The village was going to have a street party right outside our house, and in doing her bit, she wanted to hang flags from the windows: not sandcastle pennants but duvet covers. I was mortified, but as she actively disapproved of embarrassment she didn't listen until I came up with this: "It's fascist. It belongs to the National Front now." This surprised and interested her. The duvet covers were hung, I went out for the day, but she listened thoughtfully to my news.

England was no longer England, at least not the England it persisted in believing itself to be. Twenty-five years earlier, when the news came of the death of George VI, people stopped their cars and stood to attention at the side of the road as a mark of respect. Twenty-five years later, the 2002 celebrations for the

Queen's Golden Jubilee would be like a show on which the curtain had gone up after the audience had left the building. As the Queen made her way through a lunch in each county, her progress had the definite air of a farewell tour. It was as if she were asking, Is anyone out there? And we were saying, We don't know, Missus, I mean Ma'am, we're not sure.

In 1977, England was halfway between these two points. People everywhere were eager to celebrate, and they were still in the habit of civic duty and collective responsibility. They formed committees and working parties, and strove to find original ways to mark this anniversary. There are trees, schools, bridges, swimming pools, and community centers that carry this date as their inauguration, and hundreds of plaques throughout the country commemorating a royal visit.

The England of the Jubilee committees was already changing. Faraway events were affecting the price of petrol, tripling the cost of coffee and prompting the disappearance of sugar from the shops. There were terrorists, foreign ones, who might be here (this was the time of the Red Army Faction and Ulrike Meinhof). While council members and social clubs planned their Jubilee parties, unemployment was climbing sharply. There would be dancing in the streets, the great act of togetherness, while 100,000 Londoners had recently voted for the National Front.

The 1977 charts were moody and indecisive, full of songs about not wanting to talk by bands who couldn't be bothered: "They Shoot Horses Don't They?"—Racing Cars; "Torn Between Two Lovers"—Mary MacGregor; "Another Suitcase in Another Hall"—Barbara Dickson; "Knowing Me, Knowing You"—Abba. Even the Muppets were "Halfway Down the Stairs." Otherwise, there was a lot of shrugging and sulking: Fleetwood Mac's "Go Your Own Way," Rod Stewart's "I Don't Wanna Talk About It," Hot Chocolate's "So You Win Again." They were fed up and so were we.

By May, a month before the Jubilee, punk bands were making forays into the charts: The Stranglers' "Peaches" and the Ramones' "Sheena Is a Punk Rocker," songs that were built on familiar rock models. Later in the summer, things would speed up with Jonathan Richman and the Modern Lovers' "Roadrunner" and the Jam's "All Around the World."

Elizabeth toured her domain and, like a Tudor monarch, processed along the Thames while the Sex Pistols hired a boat called *Queen Elizabeth* and did the same, playing their own "God Save the Queen." Banned by the BBC, it still reached Number One, although many record shops refused to admit that, leaving a blank space in its place in chart listings. The pressing plant had at first refused to manufacture the record and the printer to print the cover. "God Save the Queen" got to Number One not just because it was shocking but because it was a real tune. It was *catchy*. Jamie Reid's cover was more disturbing than the song itself. It featured an official portrait of the Queen in necklace and tiara, with her eyes and mouth covered by ransom-note-style newspaper text. Blindfolded, gagged, and pierced by a safety pin through her nose, she looked far more frail than she might had Reid just added a mustache and glasses. In the new England, little old ladies got hurt, even royal little old ladies.

Those who organized the street parties might have remembered the celebrations for the Coronation, or the end of the war. This celebration was taking place in the shadow of unemployment, terrorism, fascism, and punk rock. I believed then that only the young understood this, because we listened to the music, went on the marches, and had bad dreams. I didn't understand how the world absorbed and adapted to change, and that punk rock would soon be, was already being, soaked up.

I avoided the village and ended up in a nearby town with friends. We couldn't think of anything to do and so we went to look at a street party. We danced on the edge, in the rain, for a brief moment part of the national celebration of a country where people laid paper cloths on tables and strung paper flags, where bands played in the open air, beacons were lit, and everyone wore paper hats and drank from paper cups and ate ice cream and jelly, as if rain was an impossibility.

# 34

# *ELVIS EST MORT*

*On Monday August 15th [1977, the day before Elvis died] I went into a shop to get a T-shirt printed with Elvis' photo on it. The shop also printed wording on T-shirts, so I asked for ELVIS to be printed above the photo. The man in the shop teased me by asking how to spell the name, and asked who this Elvis was. I did not realise at the time that he was joking, and I replied in all seriousness.*

—TONY CLAPTON

Walking the length of the beach to buy Gauloises and a glass of *diabolo menthe*—crème de menthe and lemonade, fizzy and green and halfway grown-up—still child-invincible so walking the length of the beach alone in the dark, walking alone from the campsite to the straggle of restaurants and outdoor discotheques where they played medleys: *"Et les Cailloux chantaient"* . . . *"I can't get no"* . . . *"It's been a hard"* . . . *"Everybody's doin' a brand new dance now,"* and the slow numbers, *"Il est trop tard,"* those two boys, hippieish but cute, *"Il est trop tard pour faire l'amour,"* who wanted to dance with my friend and her

sister, whom we thought we'd see tomorrow but saw only once
more days later, by which time we'd become part of a gang who
hung around a different disco, we'd met them walking the
beach, noticing, deciding, daring each other to walk up with a
cigarette, *Vous avez du feu?* Among them the golden couple who
used me to argue with each other, and the night she wasn't there
he got me to walk into the dark and pretended not to understand when I wouldn't lie down, and yes he had a girlfriend but
what was the problem, she wasn't there and nothing was serious,
not even the letter that came later, *Ma petite Anglaise adorée*, from
him or him? Because this was a medley, all of us fifteen, sixteen,
seventeen, making it up out of bits of what we knew, and we were
free because there were only tents and the beach and the track
between the two, and we spent all day soaking up heat and salt
and planning the night, these French boys wanting me to trans-
late the words to David Bowie's "Young Americans"— *"He pulls in
just behind the fridge."* All night, barely noticing the adults we were
with, my friend's parents and her uncle and aunt, who had
brought us here and who took us for meals and corrected our
French but let us roam free. The last night, how we lay in a medley, everyone sleeping on someone else and the night darker and
colder than I thought, and we woke in a confusion of tempera-
tures to find grown-ups and children wandering past in their
swimsuits and us left behind, as if we'd slipped down a crack between them. Too clear, and we woke and walked to the end of
the beach to buy Gauloises and *diabolo menthes* for breakfast, the
newsstands: *Elvis est mort.* Late Elvis, "In the Ghetto," "Suspicious
Minds," his mansion of a voice, but lumbering, sclerotic now,
that was who had died, not the inky nimble "King Creole," the
shivery boy of "Jailhouse Rock." It didn't hurt, he was a story by
then, a double album of greatest hits someone gave me for
Christmas. We left him behind with the boys and the heat and
the medleys, not knowing what it meant to see someone like that

for the first time, to hear a voice shaped like that, a body move like that for the first time, we knew nothing yet of such disturbance and drove north, three girls in a crush on the backseat trying to sleep, and when we couldn't sleep we would be dreaming, for now of Michel or Joël, Yannick or Olivier, *Je t'aime et tu danse bien . . . mais ce soir . . . il est trop tard . . .* and it would take days to get home, the long drive and the ferry, the sea we'd cross as the sun pulled away, and we wrapped up and sank back into village life and school life and family life, and the first of the last years of it all.

# SEPARATION AND CONTRAST

*. . . color . . . exhibits itself by separation and contrast, by commixture and union by augmentation and neutralization, by communication and dissolution . . .*

—JOHANN WOLFGANG VON GOETHE,
*A Theory of Colors*

That year, Marc Bolan had a television show called *Marc*, and in the first episode he promised "a lot of new sounds, a lot of new experiences," before introducing . . . Who was it again? He picked up a badge as if to check the name and then waved an arm dismissively in their direction—"Oh yeah, the Jam." A man who sported ringlets and a leopard-skin catsuit talking in a floppy voice about three boys who buttoned down their collars and measured the turnups on their trousers. While Bolan lounged on a fluffy pink throne, the Jam posed rigidly—black suits, white shirts, black ties, black-and-white shoes—in front of a plain black backdrop. Clean-shaven, short-haired, and with emphatic estuary accents, the Jam played "All Around the World," and here was a speeded-up, pared-down sound that I knew could take me farther and faster than any boy in his car. Bolan cooed and drawled but the Jam shouted: "All around the world I've been looking for new . . ." I was looking for "new," and it lay in such collisions and detonations and two-minute songs, and in a new kind of color.

Essex in the 1970s was a world of painted pub signs rather than of neon, of black-and-white television, early closing time, and the corner shop. Children wore school uniform, men wore suits or at least jackets, women wore coordinated outfits by day and blocks of color or floral expanses on special occasions. Many in the village did not leave the house without hat and gloves, whatever the weather. Teenagers were subdued. The shape of their clothes had started changing along with the shape of their music, but for most, it happened slowly. We were so color de-prived that we were impressed by a set of six winking red, yellow, and green lights lined up in front of a DJ's deck.

In November, our English teacher took us to see *Othello* at a theater marooned in a shopping precinct in Basildon New Town, a place of concrete that looked as if it had never quite dried out. It was just another long afternoon to be gotten through, and then, as we were ushered off the bus, I caught sight in a shop window of the cover of the Sex Pistols' *Never Mind the Bollocks*. The offending word had been covered with tape but that didn't thrill me nearly as much as the bubblegum pink and acid yellow of the cover. It was strident, lurid, and magnificently out of place in that damp mall. It buzzed.

The colors of punk, like its rumor, set off a vibration and cracks began to appear—orange socks, blue hair, lime-green nails, pink trousers. Hippies wore orange, pink, and lime too, but in shades of flowers and fruit whereas the punk equivalents were synthetic. Punk colors were primary but not in terms of light theory: that meant a rainbow, which was hippie shit. A rain-bow was beautiful, softly graduated, and glistening. With punk, it was more as if an old image of the world had been broken down to the four components of color printing: cyan, magenta, yellow, and black. These are dead colors. Alone, they suck in light, but reduced to tiny dots they can be used to build up a full-color image that looks realistic. They conspire to play an optical trick, the illusion of glorious Technicolor out of three nasty shades. In punk, color combinations were dishwater and vomit. It was a form of aesthetic resistance, a spectrum chosen to remind the world of all that was unnatural or decayed: pink like rubber rather than roses, green like snot rather than leaves.

Punk didn't just change what I listened to and how I dressed. It altered my aesthetic sense completely. This is what music could do: change the shape of the world and my shape within it, how I saw, what I liked, and what I wanted to look like. How does this work? You listen to Yes and fall in love with boys with long hair. You listen to T. Rex and find only men in Lurex scarves beautiful. Or is it the other way around? That you find you like the look of boys in suits, the Jam say, and so fall in love with their songs? Does it depend who you come across or is there something building up inside you, as I believe there was in me—a half-formed vision needing an external phenomenon, such as music, in order to complete itself?

# FREEDOM

*Hawks over the sea . . .*
*As we*
*In our village dance*
*In smaller circles*
— TAIGI

In that coming of color and noise, I took a step back and found myself walking along a Suffolk highway at midnight in December. I had gone to Ipswich with three friends to see Uriah Heep. We had not thought about how we might get home and found ourselves stranded, the last train long gone. We walked back out of town to the highway, planning to hitch the fifty miles home.

The first live bands I saw were rock bands—Alex Harvey, Dr Feelgood, Santana, and now Uriah Heep. They were old-fashioned performers, men getting on a bit who acted the part so well that watching them was like watching a play about rock. Their music sounded more or less as it did on record, but the vision of them, the actuality, was scintillating. I had seen bands in black and white on TV, or in simplified color in magazines, but here was animation and brightness. I didn't care who they were or what they were playing, I was thrilled by the experience of something *live*.

I was starting to want another kind of live experience—a real boyfriend. I had been falling in love for years, carving initials, crying and dreaming, waiting all day for a particular moment when I knew I would pass someone on the stairs between classes, but that was all I wanted—the possibility. If a boy came toward me, I panicked and ran. Once or twice, I managed to say, Yes, I will go out with you, and then the boy wasn't over there but here, and not remote but eager. After a few awkward evenings he lost his charm, and I felt trapped.

Now I felt ready but the slow dancers were gone and there were only the serious boys who were my friends, and they did not thrill me. I needed boys I didn't know, and the only source was my elder brother. While I was going through a series of rapid and violent transformations, my brother was consistent. At ten he moved into the garage, at university he would live in a bus, and from there he would head for a Scottish island and, eventually, New Zealand. He exempted himself by being himself, and this made him free. But I didn't want a boy like my brother. He wore a coat he'd fashioned out of a goatskin rug and went barefoot in winter until my father bought him a kit for making his own shoes. His friends were hippies but, for a brief while, they were nonetheless a solution. They looked like grown-ups, and the girls—with their muted gestures and annoying calm—like women. I dug out my mother's afghan coat, started growing my hair once more, and acquired a quilted Indian jacket and an embroidered skirt. Joe asked me out. We did not amount to anything but went on flirting and stayed friends, and here I was with him and his friend Chris and my friend Cara walking along the Suffolk road.

I wanted the interest of boys like Joe and to demonstrate a

kind of growing up, even to try out being a woman, and so I wore the Indian jacket, burned incense, and listened to their rock. I went to hear Dr Feelgood or Barclay James Harvest at the Southend Kursaal because Joe would put his arms around me and his mouth on the back of my neck. That was what the evening was for.

I listened to Santana's *Abraxas* and Fleetwood Mac's *Rumours* in the same manner that I read my horoscope: eager for illumination, which I instantly forgot. This music was serious, or at least it was performed by people who were very serious indeed.

Being a woman seemed to mean listening to the music boys liked and neither dancing nor singing along. That would be annoying. And while the boys were serious about music, they didn't expect me to be so too. A boy could impress a girl with his musical knowledge and taste, but it was something he was showing her, like a fleet of cars or a gun collection. She was not meant to join in. Girls and music were separate pursuits. Or do I mean women? Was I a woman yet? Perhaps the fact that I was noticing such things, how boys (men?) wanted me to behave, meant that I was.

We walked on along the road. Joe found a dead pigeon and carried it for a time, singing "O for the Wings of a Dove," and we laughed more than we should have and found other things to sing. We tried to hitch and finally a car slowed down and we ran toward it, somehow not noticing that it was the police. Two officers got out. They asked us to turn out our pockets. Joe produced a bunch of a dozen or so keys.

"What is this key for?"

"The goat shed." He lived on a small farm.

"And this?"

"The chicken coop."

"You taking the piss, son?"

"And that one's for the barn."

They searched the two boys, found some grass in Chris's pocket and arrested him. One of the officers radioed for a van to come and pick us all up. The other one turned to Cara and me: "I can't search you two girls, so I'm arresting you on suspicion of possession and taking you in." The Black Maria arrived in a matter of minutes and the four of us got into the back, Chris murmuring, "Sorry, sorry," and the rest of us smiling and shrugging and saying it didn't matter. This was an adventure and anyway, we were glad to be out of the cold.

At the station, we were separated.

"Name? Spell it. Date of birth? Address? Spell it. One leather wallet containing two pounds and fifty-three pence, one eye-makeup pencil, one silver bracelet, four bead bracelets, one silver necklace, three sanitary items, four cigarettes, one Bic lighter, one bar of chocolate, one sprig of heather in foil. Where did you get this?"

"I bought it from a Gypsy in the street."

"Take the foil down to the lab, Eric, and check it for cocaine."

In Essex?

"You think that's funny, girlie?"

"Yes, no, I—"

"We need to contact your parents. You're not going anywhere without one of them. What's your dad going to say about this?"

I was sure of what he would say about this. "He'll come and get me, he won't mind. Please call him, call him now."

The officer smiled and said nothing and handed me on to another officer, larger and more gentle, who with something resembling sadness locked me in a cell. It must have been lit but to me it was appallingly dark: a wooden bench, and no windows other than a small slat in the heaviest door I have ever seen. It shut with the force of the Pied Piper closing the mountain. Had

I ever been locked in a room before—with nothing to do and no idea of when I would be let out again?

After some hours I was taken to another room where a thin, quiet woman asked me a lot of questions without looking me in the eye. Name? Spell it. Date of birth? Address? Spell it. She wanted to know about Chris and Joe. Had I been with them all night? Had they given me any drugs? I knew they were seventeen and what this meant. I had heard the phrase "dealing to a minor" and knew that it was like "having sex with a minor" and that it was serious. I said we'd only met them there and I had no idea they had anything on them. She asked the same questions in different ways, over and over, until the only ones I felt I could actually answer were name, date of birth, and address, although I was forgetting how to spell any of that.

Eventually, I was taken back to the cell. I asked the giant if anyone had phoned my parents, because they would be worrying, but he couldn't say. More time passed and then another female officer took me to a room where Cara was waiting. Name? Spell it. Date of birth? Address? Spell it. This was a larger cell with a longer bench, and it was so brightly lit that my eyes hurt. Another female officer came in. They put on rubber gloves and explained what they were about to do.

I handed over the Indian quilted jacket, the silk scarf, the Southern Comfort sweatshirt, the plaid shirt, the desert boots, the patched jeans. My underwear. I didn't look at Cara or at the women, and didn't understand when they told us to get up on the bench and jump off.

"Why?"

"We want to see if anything falls out."

"Falls out of where?"

"Of where you've hidden it."

An hour or two later, I needed to go to the lavatory and

called through the slat to the giant, who sent for a female officer because I had to be accompanied. As she stood on the other side of the brief gate to the stall, she asked me what my name was. I began to spell it, to give my date of birth, my address, but she said, It's all right, I was only making conversation. I'd forgotten what conversation was.

When my father arrived, I could hear him shouting, but at them rather than me. We were taken back to the thin woman and she asked me the questions again but this time only once. As a minor, I could not be interviewed without a parent present. My father drove me and Cara home. He said little, and was more worried for us than angry. They had waited hours before calling him, until after I had jumped off that bench, but even then they told him only that I had been arrested on suspicion of possession. He had refused to be shocked or furious, as the police had evidently hoped, wanting only to get me out of there. The next day I asked him why he wasn't angry and why they allowed me such freedom.

"Because we have tried to instill in you a sense of judgment. I hope that while you will try things, you will know where to draw the line."

But I didn't know how to draw my own lines yet. And it turned out that I still wasn't ready for a real boyfriend after all. To my brother's annoyance, I made my way through a string of his acquaintances, flirting with them till they asked me out, allowing them to kiss me and then running away. The strongest impulse I had was toward freedom. I did not have words for what I felt, and it was those songs that mentioned freedom which spoke to me most strongly. I had gone to see Uriah Heep because of their rock ballad "Sweet Freedom." I made Luke play Lynyrd Skynyrd's endless "Free Bird." I remembered slow dancing to Deniece Williams's "Free."

For all my unease and loneliness it seemed that I wanted, needed, to be free. I knew this and ignored it as much as I could, as if I knew already what it might cost. Freedom. It could mean anything. Yet when I heard it sung, in whatever way, I felt re-stored to some deep imperative and for that moment, entirely self-sufficient—free.

# 37

# PROTEST AND SURVIVE

*Your radio will be your only link with the outside
world. So take a spare one with you if you can.
Keep any aerial pushed in. You will need to listen
for instructions about what to do after the attack
and while you remain in your fall-out room.*

—*Protect and Survive*, 1980

I grew up with Vietnam as a myth in the making and the IRA
bombing campaigns as a local reality. Nuclear war was palpa-
ble as people whispered about civil emergency plans and
the first government guidelines were issued to local government
and relevant others. As my father was a doctor, he was included
in the local plans. The Home Office would later issue a pam-
phlet on how to build a domestic bomb shelter. By 1980, most
households had received *Protect and Survive*.

Even the safest room in your home is not safe enough, however. You will need to block up windows in the room, and any
other openings, and to make the outside walls thicker, and
also to thicken the floor above you, to provide the strongest

possible protection against the penetration of radiation. Thick, dense materials are the best, and bricks, concrete or building blocks, timber, boxes of earth, sand, books, and furniture might all be used.

The Campaign for Nuclear Disarmament put out a counterblast, written by E. P. Thompson, called *Protest and Survive*, which my mother left by the telephone as anyone else might a vase of dried flowers. She voted Communist, sent telegrams for Amnesty, and campaigned for Taxes for Peace. Clearly she believed we could each change the world, but what convinced me this was possible was music.

In August 1977, there was a rally in south London to prevent the National Front marching. After this, the Anti-Nazi League and Rock Against Racism brought together punk and reggae in protest events. In April 1978, Cara and I sneaked off to the Rock Against Racism carnival in London. It began with a march from Trafalgar Square to Brixton's Victoria Park. We were there for the music but also to change the world, two among tens of thousands who were going to stamp out racism and the National Front.

Punk did not save any whales but it made itself a force for change. It believed in something after all. Singing along, we believed in it too. If we could come together, make this noise, and take up this space, then surely what we had to say would make something happen. There would be no more racism, no more police oppression, no arms escalation, no war. Music, with its pumped-up feelings, fooled us into this. We felt part of something powerful and, because we all knew the words, something fantastically simple too.

I could not really conceive of nuclear war any more than I believed that as we marched through London we were actually spreading love and peace.

If you are in the open and cannot get home within a couple of minutes, go immediately to the nearest building. If there is no building nearby and you cannot reach one within a couple of minutes, use any kind of cover, or lie flat (in a ditch) and cover the exposed skin of the head and hands.

Policemen lined the route as impassively as lampposts, and behind them, behind barriers, old men in caps waved their fists or brandished copies of *British Bulldog*. There were reports of conspiracies and violence, but I saw nothing. I walked and shouted for hours and then squeezed my way into Victoria Park, where I could just about see, but not really hear, the bands. I watched them anyway—the Clash, the Tom Robinson Band, Steel Pulse, and X-Ray Spex. They mouthed and grimaced and gesticulated, just like the old men in caps. We were all protesting. We would all survive.

# 38

# LOST PEOPLE'S
# MEETING POINT

*We have, over the years, pressed for a flagpole or
something similar from the promoter to fly a "lost
people's" flag, but in the face of continuing failure
we may have to ourselves explore the cost of a large
banner saying for instance "Lost People's Meeting
Point" which we can fly over the Festival Welfare
Service tent. Given sufficient warning it may be
possible to approach local scout groups, etc. in the
hope of borrowing flagpoles.*

—JAN HITCHENS,
"Local Welfare Groups Report,
Knebworth Festival, 29th June 1978"

Somewhere among these excursions, I finished my exams
and left school. I was still fifteen, the youngest in my year.
On my last day I walked home instead of catching the bus,
knowing that this was a moment I wanted to concentrate on and
remember. I knew I would not have done well; I had made sure
of that. One morning, a distressed art teacher had called me in

to show me that someone had sabotaged my exam work. They had drawn little stick figures all over it. She could think of nothing to say when I explained that it had been me, and neither could I. When the examiner arrived he said that he wanted to give me a better grade but I had produced so little. He needed to see more and was prepared to come back. Did I have any work at home? I was sent for but wasn't in my Russian class, having played truant to get my hair cut. I took no notice of the teacher's consternation and was indifferent to the lost grade. My exams were happening without me.

That was the last of a number of ways in which certain teachers tried to help me or to wake me up, but I didn't understand this till later.

My experiments with older boys had finally led to a boyfriend, David. He was tall and graceful, a handsome man rather than a cute boy. He was far more grown-up than me, so much so that it astonishes me to think that he was actually only eighteen.

Before David, there was a run of boys who lasted a couple of weeks each, partly because when they asked me out I found myself unable to say no and so endured an awkward night in a pub. I did this with Mike, whom I saw the next night at a party, staggering about drunk.

"Idon'twanttogooutwithyou," I said by way of greeting.

"Wha—?" The music was loud.

"I DON'T WANT TO GO OUT WITH YOU!" I shouted.

Mike staggered and grinned. "Sfine, sno hard feelins, sfine . . ."

That was easy, I thought. I was direct, he was fine. It was fine. The next day, Mike appeared at the front door.

"Hello?" I said.

"Are we off then? It begins at eight."

"But—"

"But what?"

"Don't you remember what I said last night?"

"Last night?"

Somehow with David I didn't feel trapped. He let me set the pace and he did grown-up things such as sending flowers and taking me out to dinner and planning excursions. I received his kindness and courtship not so much as gifts as facts, in the way I received the facts of my own lost state. It did not occur to me that I could actively change myself or that I could, let alone should, get actively involved.

So I'd left school and acquired a boyfriend, but it was still only June. Life would not begin again until sixth-form college in September. I relied on David, who organized two trips—to Knebworth Festival and to see Bob Dylan, who was playing at Blackbushe, an aerodrome in Surrey, that July.

Knebworth was two days with sixty thousand other people in a field in the rain. We slept four to a two-man tent, and spent our time trying to get dry or queuing for lavatories that were so overwhelmed that most people took one look at them and headed off into the fields. The atmosphere was hippieish, with people being strenuously trusting and mellow. The only ones who got hurt were a pair who'd gone to sleep on a track wrapped up in dustbin bags and who'd been run over because they were impossible to spot in the dark, and even they were just badly bruised. The real threat was the food:

> After the birth of a baby at the 1976 Festival, first aiders were given a crash course in midwifery, but most of the medical problems came from the Hare Krishna free soup kitchen.

Outlets listed their prices in the program: "*(Examples)* Soft Ice Cream 15p; Yoglace (Iced Yoghurt) 15p; Fish and Chips 70p; Chicken and Chips 75p; Beef Burgers 65p; Hamburgers 35p; Tea 13p; Coffee 15p." Despite the cheapness of what was on offer, the welfare officer's report noted people running out of money and requiring free food.

> At about 11.00 pm the Welfare/Information point in the arena started dealing with cases of people who were distressed because they had lost friends. This was especially the case with people who had not made arrangements for where to meet up with friends if they became separated in the crowd. This increased until well after the concert finished, when enquiries then related to where stranded or exhausted people could find somewhere warm and dry to sleep.

The real problem was people getting lost. Information signs were few and small, as if no one wanted to do any shouting. That would be uncool. No one had a plan. We didn't know why we were there or how we were going to get home. The music had got lost too, not only because it wandered off on the wind so most people could barely hear it, but because of the bands on the bill. The headlining act was Genesis, who had recently lost their lead singer, Peter Gabriel. There was Jefferson Starship, whose singer Grace Slick failed to turn up. There was the jazz-fusion outfit Brand X, and after them the Atlanta Rhythm Section and Tom Petty and the Heartbreakers, famous for not quite making it here.

Up to this point, I had been more interested in being at a festival than listening to the music. I was cold, damp, and exhausted and as I couldn't really hear anything, I lay down next to David and slept. Then a band came on who had nothing to do with rock festivals or rain.

Devo wore surgical outfits, as if setting up a sterile field in order to protect themselves from these filthy English hippies. They had short hair and sang in clipped syllables, and their music and dancing were restless, aggressive, and smart: "Are we not men? We are Devo!" They were a wonderful irritant, especially when they did a cover version of the Rolling Stones' "Satisfaction" that stole the song entirely, turning its machismo into neurosis. The audience was enraged and for a moment actually reacted, pelting the band with beer cans.

This was the group I'd wanted most to see, and watching them now I wondered where they came from. They were absolutely new. I don't remember seeing any punks at Knebworth but there must have been hundreds of people like me, who didn't think of themselves as hippies and didn't like rock but were trapped by the fact that those were the only languages available.

The new language was evident in the differences between set lists.

*Genesis:* "Eleventh Earl of Mar," "The Fountain of Salmacis," "Burning Rope," "Deep in the Motherlode"
*Jefferson Starship:* "Ride the Tiger," "Wooden Ships," "Dance with the Dragon," "Pride of Man," "Sweeter Than Honey"
*Devo:* "Wiggly World," "Pink Pussycat," "Too Much Paranoia," "Uncontrollable Urge," "Mongoloid," "Jocko Homo," "Smart Patrol/Mr. DNA," "Gut Feeling/Slap Your Mammy"

In front of these bands was a mass of lost English youth, confused by music that was on its way out and music they had yet to grasp and the complete lack of connection between the two.

There was an enormous amount of litter left behind, especially polythene sheeting and bags which people had slept under as shelter from the rain. It seems a pity that more of this plastic couldn't have been reused and recycled.*

*Festival Welfare Services, Field Worker's Report, Knebworth Festival, June 1978

Two months later, David took me to see Bob Dylan at Black-bushe. We caught a train to London and then traveled by Tube to Victoria. As we pulled into the station, I began to panic. The place was full of people who were evidently also going to Black-bushe. I was back in the mass of lost youth. We inched toward the platform and were herded onto an already crammed train. I apologized to David but could offer no explanation as I jumped off just before the train departed, and fled.

# 39

# A HOME FOR GOOD MUSIC

*I require clothes and money, that is all. These are*
*easy goals that do not disturb one's sleep.*
                        —HERMANN HESSE,
                        *Siddhartha*

So it was possible to organize—to ring up and speak to someone in a box office, to send a postal order, an SAE, and to arrive with tickets, to have planned an evening out. Like using a bank account or returning something to a shop, this is one of those adult procedures about which you gather clues until you feel confident enough to have a go on your own. In the first few transactions you will be conscious of enacting adulthood, and will speak as if in a foreign language, getting the tone wrong and not understanding the shorthand.

I read the listings in the *New Musical Express* and persuaded Cara to come down to London with me to see the Vibrators play at the Marquee Club in Wardour Street. I had only just heard of the band, but the club and the street were famous.* I also invited

---

*"Where is the pop corner of the world? For thousands of youngsters it is London's Marquee Club. It is the melting pot of today's hip music, where jazz, folk, and pop meet on equal

Beth, a girl from Ohio with whom I'd been friends as a child. Against all the odds, we had kept up a correspondence from the age of ten and now she was passing through London again. Like a grown-up she rang and asked if we might meet, and like a grown-up I thought about how to entertain a visitor and invited her along.

We arranged to meet at Tottenham Court Road Tube and walked along Oxford Street chatting politely before turning into the darkness of Wardour Street. To my relief, we looked more or less the same: fresh-faced and wearing jeans. Where was the club? I was expecting a hall, lights, and a long queue, but there was nothing except a small sign sticking out into the street like that of a minicab office.

A narrow corridor led to some stairs. To go in, we had to become members and so bought "Privilege Cards." I still have mine, which I kept perhaps because it seemed like a credential— a small blue card in a plastic wallet, expiring on December 31, 1978. "Not valid unless signed," it says, and that is where I let myself down. The dots above the *i*'s in my name are looped circles.

I led the way downstairs, confident of what I was walking into. I had been to see bands, after all. Only here was a room with as much atmosphere as an office. It wasn't dark, just dingy, and the stage was somehow so unobtrusive that the band seemed to play in front of rather than above you.

I had never seen a band play without performing before. The Vibrators just got on with it, as did the audience. There was no rapt attention, no sense of event, no light show, dry ice, cheering, or applause. I loved it and was enjoying myself until I noticed that most of the other girls there were wearing garbage

---

terms. Where trends are born, and stars emerge. It could be compared with New York's Apollo Theatre, but really there is nothing like it in the world. Music is the important quantity at the Marquee, and the club-goers are London's most aware, adult teenagers. The Marquee is a home for good music." —*Melody Maker* (Marquee Club program, 1968)

bags. We three were the only ones in jeans, and while I was taken aback, I was not particularly agitated. I felt invisible, as if I could wander through this scene untouched because I was beneath notice. And that is what I did. I forgot about Cara and Beth, and explored the dark corners, observing how these people stood and talked and moved. They did everything everyone else did but differently, with a kind of detraction. They took away expectation—being a boy or a girl or a member of a band meant nothing.

I considered what it would take to achieve such freedom. I could lay my hands on garbage bags and hair dye, and I could save up for bondage trousers. Money and clothes were the easy part. The difficulty lay in how not to be and above all how not to be a girl. How could I subtract enough of myself to achieve that?

Cara got bored. She had been reading *Siddhartha* on the train and decided to find somewhere to continue, so sat down in the corridor. Ten minutes later, she was back.

"Do you like the band after all?" I asked.

"No, but I'm not staying out there. Some wanker fell out of the toilets and puked on my book."

# 40

# SECONDARY WORLDS

*In the primary world, we all have experienced occa-*
*sions when, as we say, we feel like singing. We may*
*sometimes even attempt to sing, but if we do, we are*
*dissatisfied with the results for two reasons. First,*
*most of us cannot produce pleasing sounds; second,*
*even if we are professional singers, we cannot com-*
*pose a song expressly for the occasion but can only*
*sing some song that already is in existence, which*
*we happen to know . . .*

—W. H. AUDEN,
*The World of Opera*

That same week, I saw my first opera when my father took me to Debussy's *Pelléas et Mélisande* at Covent Garden. I traveled down to London and spent the afternoon with Beth, who watched in astonishment as I changed into a long floral dress. I had chosen this outfit with what was expected of me in mind. It had nothing to do with *me*. In any case, I was thrilled by the idea of going to the opera. When we had lived in London, my parents had gone often. Opera was what you dressed up for

and what my father sat up alone late at night listening to. I knew
it would give me feelings.

*Pelléas et Mélisande*, though, is elusive and suggestive, a work in
which Debussy made the decision to be deliberately unforthcom-
ing. As he explained to a friend, he had discovered "a technique
that seems to me quite extraordinary, that is to say Silence." I
didn't want silence. I wanted to be bashed over the head with
feeling.

Until the lights dimmed, the evening didn't disappoint: gilt
and velvet, diamonds and lorgnettes, the murky boxes in which
novels used to be played out. After that all I can remember is a
wash of music as a bunch of kings and queens, brothers and sisters argued and plotted and made up.

What did I expect? A secondary world that lit up the primary:
color, drama, volume, everything high. Yet here were the singers
standing around while the music piled up on top of itself and
Mélisande, up in her tower, let down her interminable hair, on
and on, yard after yard, as Pelléas waited below.

I thought of opera as sensation, I still think of it as such, and
one reason I could not sense *Pelléas* was that I could not see it.
Mine was the world of the close-up, of corners and cracks, tight
frames and vivid abstraction. Such hyperreal visuals couldn't be
achieved by people in long frocks and helmets waving their arms
on a faraway stage.

It didn't sound right either. Sometimes a wave of brass en-
gulfed the singing, or in a duet one voice overrode another and
I felt irritated.* I had assumed that live opera would look like a
film and sound like a record. I was unaware of how conditioned
I already was to experience such things in a particular way. I

---

*I once went to a performance of Benjamin Britten's *War Requiem* with a singer, Ted Huffman, and afterward complained of the difficulty of getting a coherent sense of the piece
when the sopranos blasted the tenor off the stage. Ted reminded me that this was live
acoustic music and not the digitally adjusted arrangement I was used to.

thought I was used to live performance but the bands I saw were electrified and mixed. They could create their own acoustics and be turned up or down at the flick of a switch; they were brought close through cameras and amplifiers. I had thought opera was artificial when all it was was a bunch of people making the noise they really made.

At the interval, my father suggested with great tact that we head off early to dinner. Had we stayed till the end, I might never have gone to see an opera again.

# HIGH MOUNTAINS

>      *. . . to me,*
> *High mountains are a feeling . . .*
> —LORD BYRON,
>   *Childe Harold's Pilgrimage*, Canto III

My sixteenth birthday was spent in the Alps, on my last Forest School Camp. We had pitched our tents just below the Sustenpass and spent our time on terrifying hikes along crumbling goat paths and shifting cliffs of scree, led by our wild-bearded camp chief, a man as tyrannical as he was hysterical. He prepared us for the hikes by forcing us to skitter down a steep, bald rockface. If you hesitated, he made you do it again. He was often angry, and the person he was most angry with was a French boy called Émile.

Émile was cool, and had blond curls even at sixteen. He shouted back at the bearded old man, and I was smitten. We established a gentle relationship, kissing and holding hands and sleeping side by side. This was just right in the blue-and-white world of the mountains: to be pleased but not disturbed.

We were camping under sunshine in snow, and if I walked a few hundred yards away from the site I could be alone in silence and whiteness. I would watch the mountains enlarge and accumulate, and adjust myself. I knew nothing grander than the Welsh hills and the cliffs of Cornwall. Mountains were a feature of fairytale geography, a world of heightened senses and heightened choices. They were also a trial: jagged peaks that had to be passed through by any questing knight or runaway princess. The landscape had such an epic scale that you could measure only in centuries and histories, the big pictures and big stories, and there was room for them all. It wouldn't have surprised me to see pilgrims on donkeys, Hannibal with his elephants, Charlemagne with his army.

I couldn't see this mountain, though, because I was on it. My memory is of a series of parts: the dirty ice, a field of snow, a fall of scree, a frozen stream, a terrifying path. We walked to the Steingletscher, the glacier, and I was shocked by how grubby, dingy, and soggy it was, how roughly put together. I had envisaged a glossy lozenge of pure blue ice. Around the campfire, we sang the usual songs from the FSC songbook: protest, folk, and blues.

Back at our tents, we sang the songs we'd left behind with our radios and stereos. I had happily forgotten my family, boyfriend, and friends but I craved music so much that I would have sung anything.

Just above our campsite was an inn where the local shepherds drank. It had a few guest rooms, and we would pool our money, buy a couple of beers among six of us, and then take it in turns to sneak upstairs to use the guest bathrooms. We even managed to smuggle in towels and use their showers.

After a few nights, the shepherds approached us. Dark, bristling, and unsmiling, they lined up. I pushed my towel out of sight.

"English?" One asked.

I nodded: Yes, English.

Their faces cracked open and one stepped forward. "My bonnie lies over the ocean . . ."

Another joined him: "My bonnie lies over the sea."

They all knew it: "My bonnie lies over the ocean. Oh, bring back my bonnie to me."

We leaped to our feet: "Bring back, bring back, oh, bring back my bonnie to me, to me . . ."

I had tears in my eyes. This song meant nothing in particular to me but it was a chance to sing. Émile wasn't David, but he was who was there. The point of it was feeling—high mountains of feeling.

# 42

# DIASTOLE, SYSTOLE

*Repeat that, repeat . . .*
—GERARD MANLEY HOPKINS,
"Fragment 14b"

When we were twelve, fourteen, sixteen, and eighteen, the house acquired a constant beat. *Will you turn that down!* There was always music coming from somewhere and we stole music from one another as we stole clothes, cigarettes, and friends. *Will someone answer the door!* Oh look, a center parting! You'll be wanting the hippie. He's in the brown room at the top of the stairs listening to that nonsense about flying teapots. *Someone answer the door!* Are you her boyfriend? She's got a boyfriend! Come in . . . No? You want to wait out there? I can tell you now she's going nowhere till she gives me back my raincoat. There she is and look, my raincoat. I know it's Dad's, technically, but he hasn't worn it for about thirty years and I took it first. No, Mum, I will not take fucking turns. It's mine. She copies everything. Look at her. Why can't we be in the living room? I'm entertaining, aren't I? Tell him to turn his music down too! It's coming through the walls at us—*Dark Side of the* fucking *Moon.* Blame him. Why didn't you knock? You should knock. No, we don't want to go to the pub with a bunch of hippies. I mean we might go, but not with you. *If you don't turn that down right now I will rip the wires out of it.*

My sister was early-morning radio, my little brother after-school television, my big brother whale song and guitar. They were to become an immunologist, an astrophysicist, and a marine biologist turned engineer, picking up on the other kind of music we grew up with. He's had twenty-five broken bones. *Osteogenesis imperfecta.* As a baby, he couldn't digest anything. *Blocked pyloric sphincter.* Why do you have blue eyes when I have green? *Heterozygous genes.* She's resting. *Supraventricular tachycardia.* The heart is *diastole* or *systole.* I am *ulna* and *radius, neuron* and *lymph, ileum* and *cerebellum.* I *exsanguinate.*

*I told you to turn it down!* I can't believe she's done that! Can you mend it? I'll buy you a drink. Yes, I know that means I'll have to go to the pub with you. Mum! We're going to the pub. *If you're all going, you must take your little brother.* He's twelve years old! *Take him.*

# 43

# A CERTAIN DISORDER

Bert van de Kamp: *What is your trademark?*

Martin Hannett: *A certain disorder in the treble range . . .**

T he principal of the sixth-form college ushered my father and me into his office. He sat down behind his desk and pulled out a packet of Lucky Strikes.

"Do you smoke, Miss Greenlaw?"

"No," said my father, "she doesn't."

One of the first people I spoke to at the college was the sharp boy called Tom. He was my brother's age and I had seen him across rooms for a year or so. He was one of those who made a concession to punk as fashion. He spiked his hair and wore a leather jacket but stuck to jeans and the Rolling Stones. Even this half measure had a powerful effect on me. He was halfway toward the kind of boy I was realizing I wanted to be with. We

---

*First published in *Muziekkrant Oor*, September 1981, in the Netherlands. Interview by Bert van de Kamp. Translated by Hans Huisman.

flirted and, probably as part of the flirtation, he borrowed an essay. He returned it as if it were something he had come across by accident and wished he'd never seen. In almost any other situation, he would have seized on this chance to humiliate but I watched him hesitate and decide to say nothing. I read his face exactly but I too said nothing. What could I say? *I knew when I was writing it how bad it was. I don't know how to think or how to talk about what I think. I haven't learned anything for years. I don't listen. I can't speak. I am watching myself happening or not happening. I watch myself and I can't, or won't, do anything to help.*

Things did not improve. My attendance record for my A-level year shows that I missed an entire term's worth of classes. I read all the French and English books on the curriculum, and was still making my way through every novel and book of poems on the shelves at home, but my habit of not absorbing and so not learning was still too strong, and it became if anything stronger as I was drawn into a group that operated rather like a teenage girl gang, through toughness, mockery, and exposure.

Sophie was a tall blonde in my English class who had a face like a Nordic goddess but wore her hair too carefully. She looked both cool and prim. Tom was pursuing her, too. One day after class she introduced herself: "You know what? You can have him. I'm not interested." And neither was I. From that moment, Sophie and I were best friends.

Tom stayed friends with us both and we formed a gang with Robert, a boy with the kind of skinny-misfit looks that punk made desirable, and another girl, Julia, who, like Sophie, was so beautiful and feminine I had not thought her interesting.

I decided it was time to draw the line and began by finishing with David, who had just shaved off one side of his hair. I then went to get my hair cut off. Sophie, Julia, and I skipped class, bought a bottle of wine, and went to the hairdressing salon upstairs in the clothes shop Miss Selfridge. This was a girly shop—

its logo was a lipstick kiss—but the hairdresser was excited by the
idea of doing her first punk cut. She turned up the music and let
us pass the bottle of wine back and forth and reduced my long
shaggy layers to a spiky crop. I walked back through town feeling
lighter. A boy called out "Punk!" and I was thrilled. The pleasure
was more than that of being different. The boy had meant to be
insulting and another time might have shouted "Slag" or "Cow."
But "Punk" had nothing to do with being a girl. It neutralized,
rejected, and released me.

I made myself strange because I felt strange and now I had
something to belong to, for which my isolation and oddness
were credentials. Suddenly the lanky boy with spots and bad
teeth was sought after; the fat girl was a goddess in garbage bag
and chains. For years I had hated being so pale; now I made myself paler. In that little Essex world, there were so many taboos
that it took little effort to break them: buy clothes from a jumble sale, men's clothes—pinstripes, cricketing whites, vests, ties,
belts, and braces.

I was reversing out of being a girl, perhaps in the hope of re-
gaining the freedom of my tomboy childhood. I stole my father's
fifties coats and suits, a school blazer from my younger brother,
and my ex-boyfriend's leather jacket. It was as if I were borrowing
a little bit of masculinity from each.

We traveled down to London to buy synthetic, metallic,
graphic tat on the King's Road, and to peer through the windows
of Vivienne Westwood's shop, Sex. In the spirit of appropriation,
adaptation, and do-it-yourself, I was constantly on the lookout for
something that could be cut up, ripped apart, dyed, bleached,
and pinned back together. I didn't want to add up. I didn't want
to form an argument or make a point. I had a weakness for the
then fashionable term *eclectic*, but the outfits I put together were
just plain odd: thirties men's flannels with a brick-red cropped
Chanel jacket and a Victorian silk shirt with a lace collar and

cuffs that was so fine I shivered putting it on; skintight plastic trousers bought from Chelsea Market, with my great-uncle's World War I leather flying coat—so enveloping and brown that it was like walking around inside a cow. Then there would be chains, scarves, badges, gloves, and lurid, shapeless garments knitted out of synthetic mohair on the biggest knitting needles I could find.

As I grew even more guarded, the colors I wore became more subdued until most of the time I just wore black. I had already dyed my hair black, which did not suit me, and then bleached out streaks that I tinted aubergine or peacock blue with Krazy Kolor. Whatever clothes I had that weren't black, I dyed. This alchemical process involved bringing gallons of water to boil in the cauldron (my mother's enamel preserving pan) and then adding the dye by piercing a tin and releasing its concentrated acrid powder. As I added salt and stirred in the clothes, a bitter cloud of steam filled the room and it did seem as if I were performing a spell that would dissolve me and my world into shadow.

Perhaps I wanted to be shadow. Certainly I did not want to be known, but then I barely knew myself. I was still a child in that I operated instinctively, and while I could be horribly talkative, on certain matters I was mute. I was discovering the pleasure of belonging to a different kind of gang in which name, appearance, sexuality, and personality were so confusingly and overtly constructed that we were all strangers. Identity was worn rather than embodied. We were keeping ourselves apart and it was a respite from becoming, and having to be, clear.

# 44

# FORGET ME NOT

*Thy mouth was open but thou couldst not sing.*
—GEORGE HERBERT,
"Death"

Something prompted me to dress up, just once, as a woman. It was May 1979, the night of Tom's dinner party, and I had met the boy with whom I was to fall fully in love. This would surprise me, as I spent my time being ironic and I didn't know how to have feelings without ironizing them too. My diary, which consisted of terse factual entries, shows that I was attempting a cultural life but also feeling grown-up enough to return to childish things like sledding, picnics, and going to the zoo.

FEBRUARY 2: SID VICIOUS DIED OF HEROIN OVERDOSE. DAVID'S HAIRCUT.

FEBRUARY 18: SLEDDING AT HEATHER HILLS

FEBRUARY 21: WENT TO ART EXHIBITION IN CAMDEN TOWN

FEBRUARY 22: WENT TO SEE JON'S SQUAT

FEBRUARY 23: TOOK JANEY TO SEE BEDROOM FARCE

FEBRUARY 25: WENT SWIMMING FOR THE FIRST TIME IN
   ONE AND A HALF YEARS

FEBRUARY 26: FELT REALLY SICK

MARCH 1: MARCUS'S PARTY. WALKED TWO AND A HALF
   MILES THE WRONG WAY.

MARCH 5: *PRIME OF MISS JEAN BRODIE*

MARCH 11: THE UNDERTONES AT THE CHANCELLOR HALL

MARCH 16: *JUST A GIGOLO* IN COLCHESTER

MARCH 21: DENTIST—GOT BRACES

MARCH 31: DIANE'S NEIGHBOUR'S PARTY

APRIL 22: COLCHESTER ZOO AND PICNIC

MAY 3: *THE LAST WALTZ*. CONSERVATIVES WON.

MAY 13: PENETRATION AT CHANCELLOR HALL

Daniel was an art student at college in Colchester who had
gone to school with Robert. We'd talked for five minutes outside
a pub. Things were whispered and I knew that Daniel knew that
I was interested. The boys sneered but Tom arranged his dinner
party so that we were both there, and made clear his expectations. It was like being given the steps to a dance and forced into
a performance. We would be part of the entertainment.

Until this point my romantic feelings had been intense but
somewhat soft at the edges. Beginnings and endings were fuzzy
and incomplete. This seemed a natural way to proceed, and
among my friends there had been a number of alignments and

reconfigurations without anyone feeling distressed. We were
plastic, our feelings too, adapting and contracting without anything getting broken.

MARCH 30: DAVID'S

APRIL 5: CUT TOM'S HAIR

APRIL 18: BRISTOL WITH TOM

APRIL 21: STAYED AT DAVID'S

APRIL 27: DAVID COMING OVER

APRIL 28: TOM CAME OVER

MAY 5: DAVID'S FOR DINNER

MAY 11: TOM'S

MAY 12: GO TO DAVID'S

MAY 26: TOM'S DINNER PARTY

Tom lived in a large, dark house on the edge of a silent town
on the Blackwater estuary, at the end of a train line that trundled
through every other silent town on its way to and from the sea. I
wore a black dress and stilettos, and believed that I was doing this
ironically. It was what punk girls did. I worried about my braces
(should I smile?) but decided that they were ironic. Poly Styrene
had braces.

Daniel was being ironic too, wearing an old-fashioned pin-
striped suit and those black-and-white crêpe-soled shoes we
called brothel creepers. Tom served an ironic dinner of pink
beef and we all sat ironically at table. We got intently drunk and
Daniel ran his hand up my stockinged leg in a way that was
meant to be ironic but which shocked us both. David, the first

boy I'd slept with, was there somewhere around the table. We had shared a year of pleasure and affection, and had anyone asked I would have said, Yes, I am in love. I had not yet experienced passion and now here it was, all at once—torment, helplessness, capture, and delight. It hurt from the start. I could think of nothing ironic to say.

After dinner, Tom gave an ironic performance as Mick Jagger and then announced that he had borrowed a house around the corner where the party would continue. It was a tiny terraced house that had been fully done up by a young couple in their thirties, with whom Tom was friends. He had said he was having a dinner party but his parents would be coming home and they had said, grown-up to grown-up, "Use our place, we're away."

Twenty drunken teenagers crammed into the living room. Some made their way upstairs, including my ex, David, with another girl. I felt nothing and neither did he, seeing me sit down on the floor in a corner with Daniel. The usual things happened. Someone was sick. Someone stood on the smoked-glass coffee table and it gave way beneath him. Tom patrolled like a ringmaster, cuing and commentating: "Martine wants someone to help her lose her virginity. Pete's going upstairs with Martine. Martine's crying because they couldn't manage it." I was used to all this but also mortified because I did not want this boy to think of me as part of such a mess. I could not speak, so I sat and smiled while he talked. Eventually he stopped talking and put his hand on my thigh. I put my hand on top of his and we kissed, but quickly in case someone noticed and we became part of the circus.

Eventually we fell asleep. I don't remember us exchanging phone numbers in the morning or making any plan to meet again. I don't remember how we began or, eighteen months later, how we ended. As we walked down the street, I picked some blue flowers I thought were forget-me-nots and stuffed them into his hand. He smiled and pushed them into his pocket. Much later, his sister told me that he had put the flowers in water and she'd asked, "Who gave you those?" And he had said, "My girlfriend," as a tease of course but even so I was astonished. We never spoke of what was happening between us. We did not name it, or each other, and I always felt that if I said anything out loud that made an assumption about our relationship, it would turn out not to exist.

JUNE 29: DANIEL'S PARTY

JULY 17: DANIEL

JULY 20: DANIEL

# 45

# THE ELECTRIC BALLROOM

*Three hundred and forty-two wax candles lit and*
*heated the room. The great crystal chandelier in the*
*middle bore no fewer than forty-eight alone. Each*
*little candle flame was reflected a thousandfold in*
*the burnished oval of the dancing parquet, making*
*it appear as if the floor were lit from below.*
                                            —JOSEPH ROTH,
                                    *The Tale of the 1002nd Night*

Crammed together in the club under the stands of the
football ground where Eddie and the Hot Rods had
played, we drank, kissed, fought, and collided, but never
got to know one another. We never knew who the band was either, as nobody famous played there. Why would they? Instead
we had Anorexia, the Urge, Modern English, Prag Vec, Essential
Logic, the Pack, Special Duties, Deep Throats, Swell Maps, Wax-
work Dummies . . . whoever it was would play for a while then fall
off stage into the swirl of that dark, low room. The village-hall
disco was an eighteenth-century ball by comparison.

This was our ballroom. When we wanted to see famous

bands, we went to famous places: Adam and the Ants, Wire, and
Joy Division at the Electric Ballroom,* the Human League at
Hammersmith Palais and again at the Lyceum.†

The Lyceum was run down but still splendid, although we
thought nothing of its domed and garlanded glittering ceilings,
its swagged curtains and plush seats or the tiny lamps that glowed
between us as we sat in the circle drinking plastic glasses of beer.
On stage, two members of the Human League, four men with
synthesizers, suddenly moved out from behind their machines
and sang "You've Lost That Loving Feeling," a cappella, and I
thought, This is what I want, not to stand around trying not to
show anything. I wanted that loving feeling and to admit what
this could be: sitting under a golden ceiling next to a boy in the
dark, just a small light between us.

We loitered on dance floors and leaned over balconies, but
most of the parquet, pillars, banquettes, and chandeliers were
gone. Instead there were striplights, spotlights, linoleum, and
emergency-exit signs. No romance could be played out because
there were no cues to act, no signals to interpret, no choices to
be made, at least not in the way they had been back in the days of
formal dancing. Back then there were things that could be said
and a certain way of saying them. We arrived at the ballroom
without dance steps, let alone a card on which to pencil in the

*The Electric Ballroom had been a Masonic lodge complete with steam room and pool, and
then a dancehall called the Buffalo, famous among the local Irish as a place to meet a mate.
Even after it became a music venue, it was popular for Greek weddings.

†The Lyceum had been the site of an eighteenth-century proto-gallery, out of which developed the Royal Academy. The theater was variously a music hall, a circus, and most famously,
Henry Irving's home:

> It is one of the prettiest houses in London, and, while large enough to enable the
> poetical drama, even in the case of the heaviest Shaksperean play, to be effectively
> mounted, is not too large for the requirements of a modern audience. It may be
> noticed that evening dress is more commonly in vogue in the stalls and dress-circle
> here than at other theatres, but there is no absolute rule. It is worth notice, too,
> that the Lyceum, occupying a perfectly isolated position with a street on each of its
> four sides, offers special facilities for egress in case of alarm . . .
> —CHARLES DICKENS,
> *Dickens's Dictionary of London, 1879*

names of boys who'd asked us to save the foxtrot or the cha-cha
for them. We were in the dark.

Punk had made its way smoothly out of the backstreet clubs
and into these dance halls. Bands settled into tours and arrived
regularly at our town halls, universities, and cinemas. I saw the
Pretenders at Essex University and the Pop Group at the University of London. The Buzzcocks and Siouxsie and the Banshees
came to the Chelmsford Odeon, where we were told not to
dance in the aisles by the old ladies who usually sold ice cream.

Maybe the punk girls didn't bond so much because they
didn't dance. That was left to the boys, lurching around in their
bondage trousers and bouncing off one another. If girls went to
the toilet to giggle and conspire, they would find some boy snort-
ing speed or doing his makeup. I admired the girls who were ag-
gressively sexual, but I couldn't be like them. The queen of the
local scene was called Rat and she was a *girl.* The spikes of her
sugar-blond hair were tipped in candy pink. She was so sweet. I
remember seeing her emerge from the club walking daintily
among puddles of vomit and urine, wearing a white muslin top
without a mark on it. She looked as if nothing could touch her,
and this is what I envied most—I wanted to look untouchable.

Punk, according to the music papers, was dead. Yet, in Essex,
spiky hair and plastic trousers caused fear and outrage. The local
police, who must have been bored, routinely turned out in riot
gear. As the teenagers spilled out of the Odeon, some looking
for the parents who'd come to pick them up, the police pushed
them up against walls, prodding them with batons until someone
reacted and then that boy, always a boy, would be taken aside.
One friend was beaten unconscious. The most terrifying experience I had was being caught up in a battle after a punk band
played in a small town on the coast where local men decided to
surround the hall and beat everyone up, starting with the girl on
the door. The police arrived but stayed in their cars and watched

as these men, some of whom had bottles and knives, set about a bunch of kids who dressed differently and dyed their hair, as if ridding the town of demons.

We were stopped routinely but I felt immune—mostly because I was young but also because I was a girl, which was odd given that I felt additionally protected by the fact that I didn't look like one. I would walk through town late at night, and if men called after me, it was in mockery rather than pursuit. To most of them, a girl with blue hair was not a girl at all.

Yet I needed a ballroom. I had been disarmed. I was not in a circle of girls and nor was there any way to dance with boys, so it was hard to get close to either. I needed some kind of dance and our music wasn't helping. As I stood next to Daniel on the floor of the Palais, nodding along to the Human League, I thought of the women who would have waltzed, been waltzed, around that room. If only I knew how to let that happen. If only he knew how to ask.

And then one day, out of nowhere, something like a waltz:

> *"Why don't you love me?"*
> *"That's assuming I don't love you."*

I wrote it down but failed to note who said what, and that I can't remember.

# 46

# SPIRAL SCRATCH

*Plastic . . . is in essence the stuff of alchemy . . .*
—ROLAND BARTHES,
*Mythologies*

The greatest act of love was to make a tape for someone. It was the only way we could share music and it was also a way of advertising yourself. Selection, order, the lettering you used for the track list, how much technical detail you went into, whether or not you added artwork or offered only artwork and no tracklist at all, these choices were as codified as a Victorian bouquet.

We also made tapes from each other's records because records were expensive. What music we owned was limited by what we could find and what we could afford. I saved up for records, read about them, dreamed about them, waited for them to come out. When I really wanted an album or single, I wanted it properly, which meant on vinyl and in a sleeve. An LP was something of substance and vision. It was not a pocket-sized rectangle containing a small brown coil wrapped in shrunken graphics.

We lived in each other's bedrooms because it was there we could play music. We went to what gigs we could, and watched television and listened to the radio, waiting to hear something we loved or for something new to thrill us. Only with records and tapes could we control what we listened to and when. Outside of our bedrooms, we had to take what we could get, when it came into earshot: a song on a car radio or being played in a shop.

Records meant even more to me than the books I cherished, but I was careless with both. They were to be used rather than looked after, and so the books got creased, torn, and stained, the records scratched. A scratch on a record is not something you can get used to. You know exactly where it will come and if the stylus will stick. This was annoying but, to me, records were an admixture of music and vinyl: I expected to hear both.

With my old box gramophone I could stack up singles, which would drop one after the other onto the deck. Disco was all about singles whereas rock was the album, the double album, the concept album, the triple concept album and not songs but "tracks." Punk brought back the single but played with every aspect of it. There were double A sides instead the traditional A and B sides, and EPs rather than LPs. Singles were as important as LPs, if not more so, and were given cover artwork. They had traditionally come in plain white or discreetly logoed sleeves but in 1977 came Devo's "Satisfaction," featuring the band trussed up in rubber blankets and wearing operating masks, and from Virgin the Sex Pistols' "Pretty Vacant," covered in splintered glass and newsprint. Colored vinyl was introduced but fell flat, as its refusal of light hurt the eyes.

The record shop was no more than a corridor squeezed into the high street. The manager, Terry, was a mild man in his thirties who knew so much about music that he didn't need to talk about it. His secondhand section was full of the bands we were just discovering and connecting to what was happening now, and so the organization of his tiny shop reflected the way in which music adds up and how it moves in cycles. The disco and prog rock relegated to the bottom shelf of the secondhand section would one day be rediscovered just as I was then following the Sex Pistols back to the New York Dolls and the Velvet Underground, and there they were on Terry's shelves.

I bought two Velvet Underground LPs as soon as I found them and was accosted in the pub a week later by Gary, a boy with new crusted piercings, hair still a bit too long to stand up, a leather jacket, some chains, but cowboy boots and jeans.

"You bought my Velvets!" he said, outraged.

"You sold them."

"Yeah. But. They're mine."

Selling records to Terry was like pawning a wedding ring or your grandfather's medals. It raised cash but the things still belonged to you. You expected them back. Even now when I play those Velvet Underground LPs, I feel as if I ought to ask Gary's permission first.

After class I would go to the shop to see what was new and just to hang around, smoking and listening, flicking through the records and enjoying the atmosphere they contrived. There were always several people in the shop, discussing music. The talk was expert, competitive, savage, and infatuated.

Often I was the only girl but I had yet to think that that had any implications. I knew there were those for whom music was soundtrack and those of us for whom it was, well, *music*, but didn't notice that most of those who took it seriously were boys. Sophie and Julia each had a few records but they didn't get upset or excited about bands. I was thrilled by discovery, crushed by disappointment, and mortified by any misplaced enthusiasm. I declared allegiance, took a position, and always had a view, not noticing that girls were bemused and boys found me boring. Was a girl not supposed to feel so strongly, let alone want so much to possess and know something for her own sake? Tom was caught too firmly in the Rolling Stones and Robert seemed more interested in the clothes. Daniel was connoisseurial. We lay on his bed listening to Ornette Coleman or Pere Ubu as he discoursed on Joseph Beuys. Everything about us was difficult—we made sure of it.

Living in a village eight miles out of town, with no friends within walking distance, I spent a lot of time alone. I was negotiating love. I read on through the books on the shelves and listened to music with total engagement. I might have the radio on when in the bath or doing homework, but listening to records required concentration. I listened and, not able to manage my own feelings, had instead the feelings of the songs.

Too old for pop posters, I pored over record covers looking perhaps for someone to be. There was a girl in a rustly bustly dress on the cover of Adam and the Ants' *Dirk Wears White Sox* whom I admired because she was evidently walking away fast and, I knew, would be dressed like that ironically. There was some fuck-you nudity: Patti Smith standing topless with her back to the camera, confronting her all-male band, or the Slits on the cover of *Cut*, wearing loincloths and covered in mud. This wasn't sexy, it was magnificent. All those songs about hurting and waiting and pleading, all those singers who mimed heartbreak and seduction, who glittered and melted, had confirmed for me the difficulty of being a girl. I could not take my clothes off like Patti Smith or the Slits, but I wished I could. Their version of girldom was, like their music, all about confidence, and it worked.

In 1980, irony imploded. Beauty and atrocity were played straight. Cupid and a starving child, who in punk would have been juxtaposed, each stood alone. The cover of Joy Division's "Atmosphere" was a photograph of snow and woods. I found its openness heartbreaking.

# 47

# FOREVER YOUNG

*What a life.*
*What a time.*
*What I felt. Then. Gone.*
—ALI SMITH,
*Hotel World*

The day Margaret Thatcher came to power in May 1979, I went to see *The Last Waltz*, Martin Scorsese's documentary of the Band's final concert. Here were Van Morrison, Joni Mitchell, Bob Dylan, Eric Clapton, Muddy Waters, and Ringo Starr, and I somehow couldn't see any of them. The only person I knew immediately was Neil Young, because of his voice, which sounds like that of a tinned cat. I had been told by my friends that this film was momentous, but came away with the impression of a lot of mumbling and shuffling. Yet I disliked most films about music precisely because they seemed so contrived.

In 1976, Thames Television broadcast *Rock Follies*, the story of a girl band. It was soap opera and rock opera in one: low-budget gritty drama played out in bedsits, squats, pubs, and rehearsal rooms combined with fantasy musical numbers. Their dreams and slogans were no less cheesy, no less naïve than those of the Partridge Family, but coming out of English mouths, from women who cropped their hair, shared lovers, rode motorbikes, and chatted while lying naked in the bath, they didn't sound so bland. At fourteen I loved *Rock Follies* and wanted to be any one of those women because while they had boyfriends and mothers and money problems, they also had one another and music, and they would walk away from anyone, no matter how much they loved or needed them, in order to make music. Could music give me the strength to do something like that?

The band was called the Little Ladies and made it into the charts, only I knew they weren't real and, in any case, the music was the worst part of the show. It was terrible, doing its best to sound like rock but made out of the same stuff as the stage musical. It belonged as firmly in a show as real pop music didn't.

Watching bands play on television was mostly disappointing. The experience was never as good as going to a gig or listening to a record, but hovered uncomfortably between the two. There was one "real" music program, *The Old Grey Whistle Test*, filmed in a studio that looked as if it was built out of plasterboard held together by insulation tape. It was like a cross between a boiler room and a gym, with no attempt made to hide its fuse boxes, ladders, and looped cables. It worked because it was doing its best not to be a show. You never noticed the lighting or any special effects, and the presenters were casual and low-key.

Film added nothing to music; it took something away. Even the most straightforward documentary took on a narrative and then it would seem as if everyone was acting. I wanted to see *Woodstock* and *Gimme Shelter* because they were about historical events—epic rock festivals where people took acid and rolled around naked in the mud, where babies were born and someone got shot. I was watching, not listening.

These films struck me as American: outdoors, pioneering,

and collective in ways of which the English were incapable. We made films about music the way we made films, so that even punk, in *The Great Rock 'n' Roll Swindle*, ended up as a kind of Ealing comedy.

I sat through *The Last Waltz* wondering why I was there, but even under such circumstances I could be caught out by a song. "Forever Young" struck me as a serious warning. Not knowing the words and forgetting all about the bunch of hippies who'd performed it, I held on to that phrase: "May you stay forever young." I was almost seventeen and for the first time I felt as if I were not young but as if I had been young and had not noticed.

# 48

# PUNK EST MORT

*The outer shell, the masonry, seemed rather to en-
close the future so that it was an electric-like shock,
a definite nervous experience . . . to cross that
threshold, if it could be so called . . .*

—F. SCOTT FITZGERALD,
*Tender Is the Night*

The whole lot of us decided to go to Paris and then Daniel
collided with a car on his motorbike and broke his leg. In
Emergency they cut off the tartan bondage trousers his
mother had made for him. I left him behind and set off in my
black plastic trousers and pointed three-inch spike-heeled boots,
as if going out for the evening. The boots were killing me but I
could not admit this and so kept them on during the three-hour
train journey to Dover, the overnight ferry to Calais, and the
four-hour train ride from there.

I was armed with a prewar map of the city I'd found in a
trunk at home (a red-leather-bound book like a pocket novel)
and a camera I thought was a Box Brownie because it came in a
brown box. Tom was half French so we deferred to him and also

to his aunt's recommendation of a hotel, which turned out to be as out of date as my camera. The sheets and windows, walls and floors were gray-brown-yellow, the bathrooms even more so: they looked splashed and splattered, and sometimes they were.

We took two rooms with three beds in each and slept more or less girls in one, boys in the other. To reach our rooms, we had to sprint along corridors and up and down stairs pressing light pushes, which resulted in little more than a dim flicker. Sophie and I talked ourselves to sleep at night with stories of rape, murder, and fire.

The Pompidou Centre was three years old and on that first day in Paris it was thrilling—modern and foreign all at once. My eyes were used to brick, plaster, thatch, and concrete and here was steel and glass, and scarlet and turquoise tubes. Best of all, it was inside out. Everything that would be hidden was on display and so I could trace how it worked. I didn't think it beautiful because I could not conceive of it as a whole but I had never before come across a building (or song, or person . . . ?) that did not hide how it was put together.

We followed Tom ("He's half French! He knows where he's going!") into the night and he chose the dingiest bar in the darkest backstreet he could find. The six of us squeezed in alongside two or three mute locals, ordered beer, and looked at one another. What now? We didn't talk much. Each of us was telling ourselves that this was authentic and untouristic and rock 'n' roll. We chose restaurants in the same way, wanting above all not to fall for what was waiting for a bunch of English teenagers unsupervised and abroad. We chose the worst-looking places in the hope that they would be a local secret. Many of the bars had jukeboxes, most of which carried the Belgian New Wave hit—"Ça Plane pour moi" by Plastic Bertrand. A year earlier, Émile had taught me the words, but only to the first verse, and now I sang along too eargerly and saw myself become a joke.

Refusing sightseeing and having little money, we had nothing much to do. We spent a lot of time in the hotel, as we would in our bedrooms at home, and once went into a cinema on the Champs-Élysées because it was showing the Who documentary, *The Kids Are Alright.*

One day we decided to move out of the hotel and managed to do so. Then I decided to go home. Before leaving, I set off for the Pompidou Centre, using my map. I stood on corners and turned it around and around, unable to find streets that were no longer there.

When I saw the Pompidou Centre for the second time, I felt tired of it already. I didn't want to know how it worked, I just wanted it to work. I didn't want to watch people travel from one place to another but for them simply to appear and disappear, as they did in life. I chose not to go in and stood outside, enjoying my decisiveness. I had celebrated my seventeenth birthday in Paris. I was walking around the city on my own. Robert had lent me his Vivienne Westwood mohair top, all loops and holes, scarlet, yellow, and black. Two boys stopped and looked. One of them approached.

"*Punk est mort!*" he bellowed as the English do to foreigners.

"Punk is dead?"

"You English?"

"Yes."

"Oh. So're we. From Harrogate."

Two boys from Yorkshire shouting the news in French to a girl from Essex. I knew they were right. We could see how it worked and so it stopped working. Or at least we needed to know what next, what more?

# 49

# SPLIT THE LARK

*Split the Lark—and you'll find the Music—*
*Bulb after Bulb, in Silver rolled—*
　　　　　—EMILY DICKINSON,
　　　　　　"Split the Lark"

Punk evolved into New Wave, which suited my seriousness and pretensions. I smoked Gauloises and carried Russian novels in my raincoat pockets. The colors of punk refined into graphic blocks of red, white, and black, and homemade noise into the colder simulations of industrial electronics. Music was more ambitious, more serious, but also becoming lyrical again. Vivienne Westwood's shop, Sex, was renamed Seditionaries. Gym slips, blazers, kilts, and diapers gave way to suits and dresses. Girls started growing their hair; sugar and water were replaced by hairspray and gel.

Punk was first an idea and then an act. Musically it was unfixable as, by definition, it was thrown together and fell apart. We had got the idea now, and could scrutinize the parts. I knew too much—that music wasn't something that simply filled the air, but something constructed and transmitted. All of a sudden it mattered what it was played on. By then we had inherited an uncle's lumbering seventies stereo system, which was far more powerful than our old machine but still not good enough. Stereo equipment had to be either all of one spectacular brand (Bang & Olufsen) or customized: the amp (NAD), the deck (Dual), the speakers (Wharfedale).

There was more and more to think about. Music was produced and critiqued; it revealed influence and allusion. I read the *New Musical Express*, which was delivered to the house each week (we were allowed one magazine each, and I had graduated from *Jackie* to *Pink* to *Cosmopolitan* to the *NME*). My father, who never minded what I wore or said, threw the *NME* across the kitchen in disgust. He could not stand the prose.

Serious music criticism was then very serious indeed. Records were assessed not only musically but also according to their cultural context and philosophical connotations. I didn't understand my father's response. To me, this wasn't being pretentious but serious. That's the problem with this country, I said. No one is prepared to be Serious, especially about Art. I liked the way these critics wrote, and fell under the rhetorical spell of their semicolons, qualifications, and parentheses. Their casual appropriations, novel compounds, and elaborate metaphors spoke of a mind that believed itself equal to anything. What's more, they believed that talking about music was talking about the human condition and so pronounced on both. I admired that.

This is from *Melody Maker*, one of the other two music papers, which occupied the status of opposition parties but sounded the same. It is from Jon Savage's 1979 review of Joy Division's first LP, *Unknown Pleasures*:

> . . . At the time of writing, our very own mode of (Western, advanced, techno-) capitalism is slipping down the slope to

its terminal phase: critical mass. Things fall apart. The cracks get wider: more paper is used, with increasing ingenuity, to cover them. Madness implodes, as people are slowly crushed, or, perhaps worse, help in crushing others. The abyss beckons: nevertheless, a febrile momentum keeps the train on the tracks. The question that lies behind the analysis (should, of course, you agree) is what action can anyone take?

One particular and vigorous product of capitalism's excess has been pop music . . . It's as much as anyone can do, it seems, to accept the process and carefully construct their theatre for performance and sale in halls in the flesh, in rooms and on radios (if you're very lucky) in the plastic . . . The song titles read as an opaque manifesto; Disorder, Day of the Lords, Candidate, Insight, New Dawn Fades . . . Loosely, they restate outsider themes (from Celine on in): the preoccupations and reactions of individuals caught in a trap they dimly perceive—anger, paranoia, alienation, feelings of thwarted power, and so on . . . Leaving the 20th century is difficult; most people prefer to go back and nostalgise, Oh Boy. Joy Division at least set a course in the present with contrails for the future—perhaps you can't ask for much more. Indeed, *Unknown Pleasures* may very well be one of the best, white, English, debut LPs of the year.

Problems remain; in recording place so accurately, Joy Division are vulnerable to any success the album may bring— once the delicate relationship with the environment is altered or tampered with, they may never produce anything as good again. And, ultimately, in their desperation and confusion about decay, there's somewhere a premise that what has decayed is more valuable than what is to follow. The strengths of the album, however, belie this.

> Perhaps it's time we all started facing the future. How
> soon will it end?

These journalists used a cultural vocabulary that we deployed with the same thoughtlessness as teenage slang: postmodern (good), semiotic (?), eclectic (usually good), esoteric (v. good), mod*erne* (trying too hard), postindustrial (interesting), decadent (usually bad). Everything was intoned ironically, whether or not irony was meant. Irony protected you from accusations of sincerity—so much for being serious.

To speak of a record was to speak of more than music: it was a production and a design. A photograph was "an Anton Corbijn." A sleeve design was "a Peter Saville." Then there was the question of the mix. Until now I hadn't given much thought to producers. I'd heard of Phil Spector and his "Wall of Sound," and admired Quincy Jones's funk arrangements, but I didn't understand what it was they did. Then I read about Martin Hannett and saw his name on records by Joy Division, the Buzzcocks, and Magazine. I began to listen differently, like someone who has grasped prosody reads a poem differently. You have an idea of form and expectation and so are able to detect the ways in which the thing resists them. It was thrilling to know that the drums shouldn't sound like that or be that high in the mix but they were because this record was produced by Martin Hannett and the way he made them sound like heartbeats exploding was by using digital delay with an immediate cutoff. Did knowing about digital delay make the exploding heartbeats less magical? I don't think so.

Hannett was talked of in the music press as a genius with just the right kind of off-his-head, skin-of-his-teeth brilliance. Stories were told of his enigmatic approach: "Right, I want you to play that again—only this time make it faster, but slower." We ob-

sessed over him as football fans might the manager of the England team. Joy Division live was a big noise, but on record Hannett separated out the components of the sound as if arranging
space. I was used to the vocals standing in front of everything
else, but here Ian Curtis's voice was arterial—buried but driving
everything. It didn't sound artificial so much as if Hannett had
found an acoustic that would reveal its essence. It sounded like
Ian Curtis, only more so.

We were about to step back across the line punk had drawn.
The more we broke music down, the more it kept joining itself
up again: punk to reggae to blues to jazz . . .

Daniel and I stood around in our buttoned-up raincoats,
looking at the parts of music and the parts of ourselves. Would
we find a way to talk to each other? Could we try just talking to
each other?

> *Bert van de Kamp:* The development of electronic instru-
> ments has widened the range of possibilities drastically,
> hasn't it?
> *Martin Hannett:* Yes, but don't forget that the conventional
> instruments have not been used to their full extent . . .

# EXPRESSIVE VALUES

*. . . to have eaten of one's mother's heart and so to understand the language of birds [is] more beautiful than an animal psychologist's study of the expressive values in bird-song.*

—ROBERT MUSIL,
*The Man Without Qualities*

Sophie and I were sitting in the library filling in university application forms. Neither our parents nor our teachers took much interest, which was more a sign of the times than of any neglect. The person who seemed most concerned was a sour sociology lecturer who gave us each a piece of advice. She told Sophie that she should forget about university and do a secretarial course and me that I had native wit that would get me so far but no farther. I would probably fail.

You had to choose six universities. Someone had suggested to Sophie that she consider Lancaster.

"Where's that?"

"Up north."

"Where?" No bands came from Lancaster.

My geographical focus was the thirty-five miles between my Essex village and London. I knew Devon, the Isle of Wight, and Wales from holidays, and Sussex and Northamptonshire from grandparents. North of London there was a blank expanse and then a cluster of cities: Manchester (Joy Division), Liverpool (Echo and the Bunnymen, Big in Japan), Sheffield (the Human League). Somewhere toward Wales was Bristol (the Pop Group).

We applied to universities on the basis of what we'd heard of and then each threw in a kamikaze choice for fun. Sophie picked Lancaster and I applied to a place that wasn't a proper university to do a course that wasn't a traditional degree. I didn't want to study English, it seemed too obvious and I read all the time anyway. I was interested in art history, philosophy, politics, French cinema, and here was a modular course that offered something of each. Otherwise I chose anywhere near London, including Sussex because that meant Brighton (Mods and Rockers fighting on the beach).

We filled in our forms and took them to a teacher who said, "No, not this here, in that column there, no, you'll have to do it again." We rearranged course codes, entry dates, and what little we were asked about ourselves and went back. "It's quite simple, really. Just follow the instructions." We couldn't follow the instructions and took five forms each to get it right. We were never going to get to university.

After that it was a matter of whether or not I liked the person I saw at the interview. I went for only two in the end, deciding that Sussex sounded like too much fresh air. At London University, I arrived in the rain and my streaked hair dripped pink on the professor's desk. But we talked about Ted Hughes and Russian folktales, and he offered me a place on the spot. The woman at the polytechnic was so warm and interested that I didn't want to go home.

It never occurred to either Sophie or me to consider Oxford

or Cambridge. We despised them and were in any case not en-
couraged to be ambitious, and I at least never worked. I also
strove hard to disguise the fact that I lived in a big house and
that my father was a doctor. The Doctor's Daughter would have
gone to the grammar school. She would have been romanced by
the Landowner's Son. She would have been Head Girl and gone
to Cambridge. My mother's contempt for privilege meant that I
was not this thing and from what I saw of doctor's daughters and
landowner's sons, I believed she was right.

I extended my contempt to myself and did not allow myself
to achieve or excel in any way. This was the time when people
said reflexively, "That's so middle class," and we, the young middle classes, said, "Yeah, fucking right it is. Fucking bourgeois." To
be bourgeois was to have a career in mind, to own a checkbook,
to have a job. The bourgeois paid for their education and so paid
for their entrance into university. Then people started paying
them. They wore bad clothes, drove new cars, and listened to terrible music. In fact, music didn't matter to them at all.

I wrote essays and sat exams, although I never stopped going
to gigs. My sixth-form college reports are single despairing lines
about my ability and refusal to work. Yet I thought and read, always carrying Dostoyevsky, Joyce, or Eliot, and going to London
most weekends, not just for bands but also to visit galleries and
see films. I was lucky in that I had access to my father's books
without him telling me what to read. I was gripped by what I was
discovering and resistant to what I was taught and could not con-
nect my intense interest in the world with what was left of my
education.

A friend's elder brother was at Cambridge, and so one week-
end, out of sheer curiosity, Sophie and I hitched there to visit
him.

We arrived at the house full of adventure to find seriousness
of a kind we had not encountered before. No one laughed or

made jokes. A bean stew was portioned out. I was invited to help myself to seconds and then reprimanded for taking too much: there were four other people who might want seconds as well. I had helped myself to as much as I could because from what I could see, that bean stew was the only food in the house.

That night, we were taken to a party. We got dressed up, put on makeup, and followed our hosts out of their quiet house and through the quiet streets. This was a party? Boys and girls sitting on floors and chairs, talking. The air seemed remarkably clear. I sat in a corner of one of these well-lit rooms and noted that these girls did not wear makeup. They wore jeans, sweaters, and flat lace-up shoes. They did not talk to me or to Sophie, and neither did the boys. They might have impressed me with their austerity and made me feel ridiculous with my spiky hair and eyeliner were it not for the fact that this was a party without music. I couldn't understand anything without music, above all a party. I couldn't grasp that at all.

# 51

# UNQUIET

*. . . what I need is soothing lullabies, and I have*
*found them in abundance in my Homer. How often*
*do I lull my tumultuous blood to rest; for you have*
*seen nothing as changeably unquiet as this heart.*
— JOHANN WOLFGANG VON GOETHE,
*The Sorrows of Young Werther*

The last days of 1979: a new government, a new decade, and the prospect of leaving home within the year. Home was in trouble, only I wouldn't find out why till my father left six months after I did. There was much that I had refused to notice or had been told but would not hear.

Among my friends nothing was said but we knew that we were separating. I could feel life opening and wanted more than anything to go off into it but as yet I had no idea what life might be. I still did no work and in any exam argued in one direction and then in the other. I had unpicked my handwriting so as to render it completely unfeminine (nothing rounded) and illegible. I was warned I might fail on my handwriting alone.

I was trapped in Youth, which was different from adolescence. Youth meant being sensitive but out of control, pretentious, ambitious, and overwhelmed, having feelings too big to know what to do with, wanting every feeling to be that big, wanting others to feel big things for you and then being terrified if this came to pass. Youth takes for granted the heart's lead, as Werther admits: "I am treating my poor heart like an ailing child; every whim is granted."

Daniel and I discussed the world, but only in theory—Barthes and Foucault. We could go no further without talking about what was wrong, which was that neither of us knew how to manage what we felt.

One day we were on a coach going to see a band and I experienced a terrible shock. It was like what you feel when someone jumps out at you, a lurch of nerves, only usually it's over in a moment as you make sense of the situation (and laugh at the joke). My nerves kept lurching. I couldn't move or speak and was having difficulty breathing. My heart skittered, my bowels melted, my bones fused. Yet nothing had happened. The coach was quietly proceeding along the highway and Daniel was holding my hand. Nothing had happened, but my mind had chosen that moment to open a trapdoor in itself.

So much could not be said. Was that why my body started screaming? Daniel tried to help and he tried, too, to talk about his own difficulties, and while I wanted more than anything to hold on to him and say that I understood and everything would be all right, I was speechless. We lay in each other's arms but all we did was listen to music.

We didn't decide to stop being in touch, only all of a sudden we weren't. I longed for him to phone me but never thought of phoning him myself. Christmas passed. I watched old films late at night and wept. Why did I not contact Daniel? Nothing had been said. We had simply stepped back.

On New Year's Eve, I went to see Joy Division at the Electric

Ballroom. Ian Curtis was an epileptic whose spasmodic, quivering bursts of dance emulated fits and sometimes were fits. He was twenty-three, the same age Goethe had been in 1772 when he met Charlotte Buff, on whom Werther's beloved is based. I imagined that Werther had Ian Curtis's pathetic beauty and the same doom-laden voice. Like his idol Jim Morrison, Curtis could, through tone alone, enlarge what he sang into the epic. These young men were *alienated*; it was a word the music papers used a lot, and which I understood from Shakespeare to mean a stepping out of the human net, letting go of the human scale and finding yourself unable to function out there and unable to get back. Hamlet:

> . . . *I could be bounded in a nut-shell*
> *and count myself a king of infinite space;*
> *were it not that I have bad dreams.*

Ian Curtis spoke to me of feeling beyond what a single person could bear, of something fundamental and archetypal—not a boyfriend who wouldn't pick up the phone but a man on an odyssey who takes twenty years to come home, or a man who mourns his wife so powerfully that he enters death in order to find her. I wasn't so interested in the woman who waits. I identified with the fated hero who cannot help who he is and what he has to do. I wasn't in love with Werther, I *was* Werther, until he shot himself and took all night and several pages to die.

I was Ian Curtis, too. Watching the lightning pass through him as he shook on stage, I thought of my panic attacks, which were also electrical, a long moment of shock. I was about to go into the world and it kept pulling itself out from under my feet. Four months later, Ian Curtis hanged himself and I realized that he was not Werther but a man in pain. I wasn't twenty-three but seventeen, and I was a girl. My pain erupted into panic every time I tried to walk away.

# 52

# PING

*Ping murmur perhaps a nature one second almost never that much memory almost never.*

—SAMUEL BECKETT,
"Ping"

And then it was June and A levels and I wandered through the exams knowing already that I had lost to them. I sat at home typing out notes I didn't read, taking comfort in my typewriter. I would type anything— letters, lists, essays for friends. Typing was writing put to music— the clack of each letter, the injection of the space bar, the ping at the end of the line, the ratcheting revision of the carriage return

PING

And between exams we gathered on people's living room floors to watch Wimbledon, Borg and McEnroe, back and forth, on and on, the one year I followed it or cared, only for the endless back and forth, the carriage return

PING

And at home, the table-tennis table in the hall, so that when two people passed, they might pick up the bats and smash a ball back and forth, spin and slice for all they're worth, but unless you knew the warp and camber, the dead spot, the sweet spot, you were lost. A tiny ball ricocheting off the walls and windows, the phone, the fireplace, the floor

PING

And in the exam hall, the heat and tedium, the knowing I was lost and being too uncertain of myself to stay in one place long enough to shape an argument, too sick of myself to care about what happened next, the heat and the open windows and music drifting in, always the same song on a radio somewhere out there, "Ring My Bell," with its synthesized pulse as if happiness depended on something mechanical

PING

And time bouncing off the walls, from one side of the page to the other, a pointless way of exhausting itself

PING

And for all the changing and saving of the world, for all the not being a girl, for all the black and white of it, the rising above and stepping aside, and for all that music had carried and shaped and shown, this was the truth: the carriage return

# 53

# WON'T YOU BE MY GIRL?

*And the wave sings because it is moving;*
*Caught in its clear side, we also sing.*
—PHILIP LARKIN,
untitled, 1946

I am of that generation who were told that all was nurture
and not nature, while being brought up by parents who enacted traditional roles. My mother was cleverer and more
original than the rest of us, but said least. While my education
was left to look after itself, I was pulled up by my father for a
poor argument: "Don't come the dumb blonde," he would say.
So I thought that if a man made a statement, he was inviting a response. Perhaps my father let me hold forth because I was not
his equal. Was it, after all, that men wanted to tell women things
and not be told? Is that what my mother knew and why she kept
quiet?

I thought I had escaped being a girl but what else could I be?
I talked to boys about music and they tried to take off my clothes,
which were after all sensual—leather, mohair, muslin, silk, net,
and lace. I caught my reflection in a shop window: black raincoat

and beret, white shirt and spotted chiffon scarf. Even with my dyed and spiked hair of course I looked like a girl, and a good girl at that. And while I aspired to the fuck-off looks of Siouxsie Sioux, I had fallen in love.

Punk lyrics were the same old love thing after all—the Buzz-cocks' "Love You More," the Vibrators' "Baby, baby, baby. Won't you be my girl?" Punk wasn't just about making it new, as most bands sang cover versions: Siouxsie and the Banshees covered the Beatles' "Helter Skelter," Sid Vicious took on Frank Sinatra's "My Way." Of course music came out of itself; of course I was going to be a girl.

On June 20, I sat my last English paper (Eliot, Jonson, *King Lear*) and went to London with Daniel to see A Certain Ratio at the ICA. I had one French exam to go but essentially I was free. A Certain Ratio were boys in baggy old army shorts, with army haircuts, playing trumpets and bopping around. They had put out a single, another cover version, of a seventies funk hit, "Shack Up." Here was the love thing once more—"Shack up, baby, shack up." As they played, people unbuttoned their rain-coats and started dancing until eventually everyone was dancing and kept on dancing, and for those hours it lasted, and for some small hours afterward, it seemed possible that I might be re-leased from whatever it was that made it so hard to be a girl, or this girl, or the girl Daniel wanted.

# 54

# FUCK ART, LET'S DANCE

*And still in my dreams I sway like one fainting*
   *strand*
*Of spiderweb, glittering and vanishing and frail*
*Above the river.*

—JAMES WRIGHT,
   "On a Phrase from Southern Ohio"

That last summer at home seemed to be getting longer and longer. I'd heard about cheap flights to America, how you could just turn up at the airport and buy a ticket on the spot, and decided to go and see Beth, who lived in Columbus, Ohio. I asked Luke if he wanted to come along and he said, Sure, why not? I wrote to Beth and suggested a trip and she wrote back, Sure, why not? I don't think any of us consulted our parents.

I had told Beth my deepest secrets because, after all, she was several thousand miles away. In our eight years of correspondence we had marveled at each other's vocabulary of experience. What was a hayride? A prom? A youth-club disco? A jumble sale? When she'd come to London two years earlier we'd looked simi-

lar enough, with our jeans and longish hair, to feel at ease. She
had taken the Vibrators gig as an adventure and was amused to
hear that I had become a punk. Before Luke and I left for Ohio,
I wrote and asked her to destroy my letters.

Luke's father drove us to the airport. "Are you sure about
these tickets?"

"Yes," I said confidently. "I read about them. You just turn up
and buy them on the day."

Only there were no cheap flights. We were there at the airport and Beth was expecting us. Someone cobbled together
a route through New York and Pittsburgh, and Luke's father
loaned us the money. When we arrived in Columbus it was raining but warm, a combination I couldn't make sense of. Beth
picked us up (she could drive!) and took us back to a low, sprawl-
ing house. There was no sign of her parents, although one of her
sisters put in a brief appearance.

I changed into black trousers, black T-shirt, blue jacket. Beth
looked at me. She didn't get me. Eventually she pointed at my
plimsolls: "My mom wears those." I followed her through the
shopping malls and downtown streets, a tanned leggy blonde in
tiny cutoff jeans trailing a short, pale girl with pink cheeks and
black-and-blue hair.

Away from England, Daniel, my music and friends, I was suddenly uncertain. No one would understand that my style was
ironic. I retreated to jeans and a T-shirt, and sat in the shade
reading books while Beth and Luke sunbathed, got stoned, and
bounced with her friends on the trampoline. Eventually they persuaded me to join them and so I gave up my seriousness and
from then on smoked and bounced, ate ice cream, and lay
around with the rest of them.

One night, Beth and Luke came giggling into the kitchen.

"Beth told me about your letters," he said. "How you used to
tell her everything."

"So?"

"So I told her that I ought to see them. I mean, you could have told her stuff about me. Anything."

"She's thrown them away. Haven't you, Beth?"

Beth hesitated. "I put them in the garbage just before you came . . ."

"They're gone, right?"

What had I told Beth? Everything. All the crushes and excitements and mortifications I had left behind me might now be exposed to someone who wasn't safely thousands of miles away from my life but at the center of it. And what had I told her about Luke? Had I mentioned the brief strange phase in which we nearly kissed but then decided not to? We had said nothing, I told no one, and we were free to move past it, only I may have told Beth.

I had known that coming to see Beth would bring me face to face with a self I had dispatched along with those letters. It was why I had asked her to throw them out. She had done so but maybe only out of politeness. She didn't seem to understand the danger I felt myself to be in.

Luke grinned. "We went out to the garbage."

Beth laughed and rolled her eyes. "He made me!" Only she wasn't really embarrassed. It wasn't that important. She began to look around for her sun cream.

Luke shrugged. "They'd gone. Who's for a beer?"

I was shaking.

That afternoon, I'd come across a tape I'd made with Cara and Janey, and had sent to Beth when I was thirteen. While Beth and Luke went out I put it on and found that I could not tell which was my voice. It was as if I were in another life, speaking another language or taking part in a play. I said nothing about the tape to Beth because I had immediately erased it.

Beth's friends had cars and fake IDs. They climbed in our

windows at midnight and drove us to apartments with gunshot holes in the walls. Yet they loved their country. On the Fourth of July, I watched the parade through Columbus of majorettes and marching bands followed by a number of tanks. Tanks rolling through the suburbs! Did no one see the irony in this? Perhaps you needed more history to develop irony. Perhaps the English had too much.

I found a record shop and bought Banshees and Clash bootlegs. Back at the house, I put the speakers in the garden and played "I'm So Bored with the U.S.A." Beth wandered past.

"Listen!" I commanded. "Just listen to this!"

"Yeah," she offered. "It's really . . ."

"But listen to what he's singing. 'I'm so bored with the U.S.A.'! It's great, isn't it?"

"Yeah?"

These were teenagers who had waterbeds and bongs but also statuettes of Mickey Mouse sticking his finger up, bearing the slogan Fuck You Iran! They were not bored with the USA.

Beth's most frightening friend was a man called Ron, or sometimes John, who was said to have a warrant out for his arrest. He was older, small and bald but ice cool. His eyes were absolutely black. He took us to clubs downtown, told stories of what happened to people he cursed at school, and while he slept with Beth, he made himself my protector. One night, Ron got me into a club called Crazy Mama's. I was still seventeen and so could not enter legally. I was drinking White Russians and Brandy Alexanders, having never had cocktails before and thrilled that they tasted like Dolly Mixture, because I was missing English sweets. I reeled across the room and into a boy who was wearing a dentist's white jacket backward (Devo!). He had spiky hair and a pierced ear, and I believed I had found the only punk in Ohio. Ron came over to explain that I was under his protection and after that we were left alone. He came back to stay at Beth's,

as many people did, and the next day I emerged to find
Luke smirking outside my room. The punk was in the living
room, where he'd found a guitar and was playing "Knockin' on
Heaven's Door."

"He's American," said Luke. "They're like the Japanese and
the Germans—they're just not punk."

"The New York Dolls? The Velvet Underground? Where do
you think punk started?"

"Well, not in fucking Ohio."

It was true that Ohio was not the America I had envisaged
from Velvet Underground albums and Jack Nicholson films. We
knew East and West Coast cities, and heard their music. We knew
about swamps and prairies, deserts and mountain ranges. But no
song or film or painting prepared us for the suburban Midwest. I
passed judgment on the huge houses, cars, and supermarkets,
the lack of sidewalks, the tanks and guns, but I was dazzled by the
infinite variety of ice-cream flavors, by air-conditioning and
multiplex cinemas, drive-in burger joints and cocktails, tornado
warnings and electrical storms.

What impressed me most was the night we went down to the
banks of the Ohio River. I could not believe the veering American scale of things—that vast slow body of water that, in the dark,
abstracted itself into presence and force, and then behind us,
frail and unlikely and just as powerful, a scattering of fireflies.

In a shop window I saw a T-shirt bearing the slogan FUCK
ART, LET'S DANCE. I copied it onto the back of a postcard and
sent it to Daniel. It was the first love letter I'd ever written.

# 55

# CCD

*The ten minutes are up, except they aren't.*
*I leave the village. Except I don't.*
*The jig fades to silence, except it doesn't.*
—NORMAN MacCAIG,
"Notations of Ten Summer Minutes"

One of the last evenings I spent in Luke's room was with Daniel and Sophie, when the four of us argued about whether or not lasting social equality was possible. We were bandying Gramsci on decadence, and Dostoyevsky, and while Luke and I were pessimistic, the other two insisted it could be done. None of us knew what we were talking about but the argument became so fierce that when Sophie and I parted in the bus station we were both crying and she sobbed, "This won't affect our friendship, will it?" Perhaps we cared about the world and what was going to become of us in it after all.

However much my parents left me to manage my own education, it was a given that I would go on studying. Sophie's father had been the first in his family to go to university. Several of my friends would be the first to go in theirs because they had grants and could get unemployment during the holidays. We had no idea what we wanted to do with our lives, but university seemed like the right place to go to think about it.

The day we went to get our results, I understood that everyone else knew how to write essays and take exams. They could think clearly. I had gotten what I'd predicted, grades of C, C, and D, and as I stood there with that slip of paper, I decided that I wanted a real education after all and I knew that it was too late. My parents seemed not to mind my failure, which was a kindness, only I wanted someone to ventriloquize for me, to say "This is terrible! Something must be done!" Only Julia warned me that it might be worth retaking my exams and reapplying. When I saw Daniel, I wept and he was astonished—more so because he had never seen me cry. "I didn't think you cared," he said. Neither did I. (A couple of years later we would finally be able to talk of what had passed between us: "I didn't think you cared," he would say then, too.)

I missed my university place by one grade but I wasn't going to waste time trying to improve on things. My imperative remained to get out and back to the city where I felt I'd left myself behind. Daniel was going to art school in London. Sophie went off to Lancaster.

CCD. I played it on the piano. It sounded neither here nor there—two side steps and a toe in the future. I had to be prepared. I didn't have my own record player so I bought a cassette player and set about making tapes.

# 56

# SEVEN YEARS LATER

*Nadya remembered what a beautiful expression—
pleading, guilty, gentle—Gorny wore whenever anyone discussed music with him and what efforts
it cost him to keep a ring of enthusiasm out of his
voice. In a society where coolness, hauteur, and non-
chalance are judged signs of breeding and good
manners, one must hide one's passions.*

—ANTON CHEKHOV,
"After the Theatre"

I was leaving the hospital with my baby daughter. Her father
came to pick us up and we walked gingerly to the lift, carrying this child toward the world. The doors opened on the
ground floor and there was Daniel, on his way up to see me. He
had made a card, a delicate print of a flower, roots and all, with
the date of her birth stamped on the back. It reminded me of
the forget-me-nots, or whatever they had been, that I'd once
given him.

We stepped out into the street—me, my baby, her father, and
Daniel. It did not seem strange. Daniel had introduced us; they

once lived in the same house. It was late autumn, chill, and at five o'clock already dark. I pulled my daughter's shawl more tightly around her face and hurried to the car. Daniel followed and then waited.

"Would you like a lift?" It was all I could think of to say.

"Yes. Thanks."

The child seat was in the back and somehow Daniel ended up sitting next to the baby while I got in the front. As we drove off, I turned around to look at her. Was she really here?

Daniel leaned forward. "Actually, something awful's just happened."

"Oh no!" I had been staring at my baby, trying to grasp the fact of her.

He continued: "I was on my way to see you and I had this case of records with me, some of my best stuff. I had to change trains at Embankment and when I'd got off I realized I'd left the bloody case behind!"

"Oh no!" I said again.

"Yeah, I ran back but the doors were shut and I swear I saw this man pick the case up. He might even have smiled."

Next to him, my daughter's soft and serious presence glowed. When did I last think about anything other than the baby?

I couldn't resist. "So what was in the case?"

"For one thing, my Public Image bootleg, and that's incredibly rare . . ."

"You mean the French import?"

"Exactly. And then there was Charlie Parker live at Birdland 1949, which took me years to hunt down."

"And what about your Billie Holiday, the one where she turns up at that Armstrong gig and sings 'Do You Know What It Means to Miss New Orleans,' and she's really ill and no one recognizes her but then they hear her and they do and they go wild, you didn't lose that, did you?"

"Yes."

"I love that."

"And I had this single in there, the first pressing of Orchestral Manoeuvres in the Dark's 'Electricity' . . ."

"The unfinished black-card cover black-embossed? That was only available for about a week. I've got that."

"Yes. Well."

"And Can?"

"*Tago Mago* was in there, I'm sure."

And so we talked our way across the city until we reached a point at which it seemed sensible to drop Daniel off. My daughter, who in these first seven days of her life had been fractious and colicky, was out for the count. We'd sung her to sleep.

# Acknowledgments

"A Grope Pizzicato" draws on "Big Brass Bed: Bob Dylan and Delay," which appeared in *Do You Mr Jones: Bob Dylan with the Poets and the Professors*, ed. Neil Corcoran, Chatto & Windus, 2002. "My Papa's Waltz" appeared first in German, translated by Roman Bucheli, in *Der Neuer Zürischer Zeitung*. Some of the ideas for this book were explored in "On Punk Rock and Not Being a Girl," a paper given at the Experience Music Project Pop Conference, Seattle, April 2005, for which opportunity I'd like to thank Marybeth Hamilton, Ann Powers, and Eric Weisbard. The paper was subsequently published in *Listen Again: A Momentary History of Pop Music*, ed. Eric Weisbard, Duke University Press, 2007. "Secondary Worlds" draws on an article written for *The Guardian*. BBC Radio 3 broadcasted earlier versions of "Plaine and Easie Rules" and "As If in Space."

Homer's *Iliad* on p. 12 is in the version by George Chapman. "The Vast Night," p. 7, "Music," p. 82, and "Spanish Dancer," p. 33, by Rainer Maria Rilke, were translated by Stephen Mitchell. "Equipped with the Eyesight and Absorption of Wasps" by Osip Mandelstam on p. 71 was translated by James Greene. Joseph Roth's *1002nd Night* on p. 166 was translated by Michael Hofmann. Robert Musil's *The Man Without Qualities* on p. 185 was translated by Eithne

Wilkins and Ernst Kaiser. Anton Chekhov's "After the Theatre" on p. 203 was translated by Ronald Hingley. Osip Mandelstam's "The Staff" on p. 110 was translated by Robert Tracy. Goethe's *The Sorrows of Young Werther* on p. 189 was translated by Michael Hulse. Tolstoy's *Anna Karenina* on p. 45 and *War and Peace* on p. 90 were translated by Rosemary Edmonds. *Siddhartha* by Hermann Hesse on p. 146 was translated by Hilda R. Rosner. Roland Barthes's *Mythologies* on p. 170 was translated by Annette Lavers.

Helpful websites included:

www.westsidestory.com

www.martinhannett.co.uk

www.iancurtis.org

www.themarqueeclub.net

www.cybertrn.demon.co.uk/atomic

www.arthurlloyd.co.uk

For bringing this about, I would like to thank Courtney Hodell, Derek Johns, Paul Keegan, and Julian Loose; and Philip Gwyn Jones for bringing it to mind.

For song and dance, and talking about them, I would like to thank Rachel Alexander, Sam Appleby, Simon Armitage, Lucy Astor, Richard Baker, Franny Bennett, Margaret Busby, Kevin Chicken, Jonathan Coe, Tony Crean, Pia Davis, Emma De'Athe, Maura Dooley, David Harsent, Lesley Henshaw, Ted Huffman, Kathleen Jamie, Jackie Kay, John Kieffer, Mark Kingwell, Elena Langer, James Lasdun, Andy MacDonald, Glyn Maxwell, Stephen Page, Don Paterson, Christina Patterson, Kate Pullinger, Alistair Roberts, Alan Scholefield, Katri Skala, Christianne Stotijn, Gregory Taylor, Raphael Urweider, Ian Wilson, and Richard Wood.

Above all I would like to thank the family Greenlaw for everything along the way, Georgia Ardizzone for my further education, and Jonathan Reekie for something else.

hir that a didn't think a was anybody. Me ma grabbed me be the hair an' started to shake me an' say, a nice fool ye managed te make outa all of us, me 'lady. How de ye think a'm iver goin' te be able te houl me head up in this town again, after all them people givin' me all that money for you, an' me takin' it from them thinkin' ye were goin' te make yer mother proud? Now ye think ye can just land back in here, puttin' on airs an' graces like the rest of us weren't good enough for ye. A said nothin' an' just looked at me ma an' after she let me hair go a went out inte the scullery an' started to wash the dishes.

As soon as the wains went out te school that day, weemen started te come te our house te get lookin' at me an' te ask me what it was like te live in a convent. Some of the weemen were the mothers of nuns who were worried about their daughters an' they asked me were the Reverent Mothers cruel an' did a think that anybody could ever be happy in a convent an' did the nuns get enough te ate an' were they warm enough in their beds at night or did they really sleep in coffins an' whip themsel's an' wear chains way nails stickin' inte their flesh?

Some of the other weemen wanted to know what kine of knickers ye wear in a convent, an' did ye stap havin' periods wance ye were there, an' did ye keep on all yer clothes te have a bath, an' was it true that all the pubic hair on the body fell aff an' the breasts shrunk the minute the holy habit was put on? A set there watchin' them an' listenin' te what they were sayin' an' a come te the conclusion that there wasn't a hope in hell of me iver gettin' through te St Jude because he was bound te be booked-up solid for all eternity dealin' way all the other hopeless cases in the worl' so he could have no time for me.

Wheniver the word landed in our town that a was te be comin' home from the convent, some weemen that kept maids allowed that a would be a great kine of a

skivvy te have aroun' their houses te break monotony of their lives be answerin' all their quest about convents. Before a even knew that a was co home, three of these weemen come te our house toul me ma that she had no need te worry about gettin' a dasent job because they would be only delighted te give me a start.

In the middle of me first mornin' home me ma me that a would be better te make up me mine qu which of these weemen a wanted te work for an' outa hir sight before she done somethin' she mi regret. A went te wan that had only recently move our town an' who had two wains an' was expectin' third in a wheen of weeks because a liked wee wa an' a reckoned that the divil ye didn't know coul be any worse than the divil ye did, but he might, a wee bit of luck, be better.

Well, this woman had a gran' house, an' beautiful wains, an' six wardrobes full of clothes, two real fur coats, an' seventy-nine pairs of shoes countin' boots an' slippers, an' hundreds of kines make-up an' perfume, an' a car of hir own, an' husband that worked nearly twenty-four hours a d an' no frien's.

She didn't really want me te do any work. All s really asked from me was that a sit listenin' te hir tal an' call hir be hir first name wheniver there w nobody else about, an' admire all hir frocks, an' tell l what a thought of all the girls she used te work way l bein' jealous of hir for havin' married such a go goer, an' criticise all the big bugs in our town f cockin' their snooks at hir because she had on worked in a shop before she was married, an' tell h that she was just as good as them an' knew how treat hir maid like an ordinary human bein' not lik them, an' sit up way hir till the middle of the nigh when hir husband come home an' drove me back our house.